INTRODUCTION TO EDUCATION
Series editor: Jonathan Solity

THE CONTROL OF EDUCATION

BOOKS IN THIS SERIES:

R. Burgess: *De-mystifying Educational Research*
J. Eggleston: *The Challenge for Teachers*
M. Fox: *Psychological Perspectives in Education*
M. Heritage: *The Curriculum in the Early Years*
G. Klein: *Education Towards Race Equality*
J. Leadbetter and P. Leadbetter: *Special Children*
L. Measor and P. Sikes: *Gender and Schools*
J. Solity and G. Bickler: *Support Services: Issues for Education, Health and Social Service Professionals*
J. Tomlinson: *The Control of Education*
S. Wolfendale: *Empowering Parents and Teachers: Working for Children*

THE CONTROL OF EDUCATION

John Tomlinson

CASSELL

Cassell
Villiers House   387 Park Avenue South
41/47 Strand   New York
London WC2N 5JE   NY 10016-8810

First published 1993

British Library Cataloguing-in-Publication Data
A catalogue record for this book is available from the British Library.

ISBN 0-304-32394-2 (hardback)
      0-304-32399-3 (paperback)

Typeset by Colset Private Ltd, Singapore

Printed and bound in Great Britain by
Biddles Ltd, Guildford and King's Lynn

CONTENTS

Foreword vii

Preface ix

Part 1: Initial Teacher Education

1 The education and training of teachers 3

Part 2: Working in School

2 Your first post in teaching: probation and induction 25

3 Contracts and conditions of service 49

4 The curriculum: the background until 1980 62

5 The curriculum: the 1980s and after 80

6 Appraisal of teachers: a new policy for the 1990s 95

7 In-service training: extended professional
development 107

8 School governors 119

Part 3: Trying to Make Sense of It

Introduction 143

9 The local education authorities 1965–92 146

10 Central government policies for education since
1979 158

Bibliography 175

Name Index 183

Subject Index 185

FOREWORD

The 1980s and 1990s have witnessed unprecedented changes to the education system. These have had a dramatic impact, particularly in relation to:

- schools' relationships with parents and the community;
- the funding and management of schools;
- the curriculum;
- the assessment of children's learning.

It can be an extremely daunting task for student teachers to unravel the details and implications of these initiatives. This Introduction to Education series therefore offers a comprehensive analysis and evaluation of educational theory and practice in the light of recent developments.

The series examines topics and issues of concern to those entering the teaching profession. Major themes representing a spectrum of educational opinion are presented in a clear, balanced and analytic manner.

The authors in the series are authorities in their field. They emphasize the need to have a well-informed and critical teaching profession and present a positive and optimistic view of the teacher's role. They endorse the view that teachers have a significant influence over the extent to which any legislation or ideology is translated into effective classroom practice.

Each author addresses similar issues, which can be summarized as:

- presenting and debating theoretical perspectives within appropriate social, political, and educational contexts;

- identifying key arguments;
- identifying individuals who have made significant contributions to the field under review;
- discussing and evaluating key legislation;
- critically evaluating research and highlighting implications for classroom practice;
- providing an overview of the current state of debate within each field;
- describing the features of good practice.

The books are written primarily for student teachers. However, they will be of interest and value to all those involved in education.

Jonathan Solity
Series Editor

PREFACE

In 1963 John Vaizey, a contemporary of mine and a close friend until his untimely death, published a book with the same title as this one – *The Control of Education*. It was a collection of essays gathered into five groups, and the extraordinary and instructive point is that four out of those five sections – 226 out of 260 pages – were about money and methods of financial control. Only the last, brief section, called 'Morals and politics', ranges a little beyond finance; and even here there is nothing about the curriculum or examinations, or assessment or evaluation: indeed, none of these words appears in the index. Neither, for that matter, do the words 'governor', 'parent', 'student' or 'pupil' (though 'pupil wastage', an abstraction, does).

I opened Vaizey's book after I had given long but unfinished thought to what a book on the control of education written in and for the 1990s might contain. It was clear to me that there were now many more control mechanisms at all levels of the service, besides those directing finance. This book will have to look at the National Curriculum, national assessment and testing, national control of examinations and teacher training, and much more. Yet Vaizey was not wrong. I was an educational administrator in a large county in 1963, and his account of the main sinews of control is one I recognize, understood at the time, and knew how to work within. Yet, even then, it would have been possible to speculate about where control over the curriculum lay, or where the division of power between headteacher and classroom teacher might lie, or where control over the training of teachers lay, and much else that we shall look at in this book. The instructive point that emerges from Vaizey's choice of themes is that he and his contemporaries (for the book was much praised) considered that his themes were indeed the key, dynamic dimensions of control – those that could be and were adjusted by those with power in central government, the local education authorities (LEAs) and schools in order to achieve progress. The other dimensions lay within an agreed and unexamined tradition, consensus, subconscious – call it what you will. It did not strike Vaizey and his contemporaries as odd to leave them as substrata, upon which one stood while looking at the changing landscape and weather that met the eye from day to day in the politics of education.

There is an irony in this. Looking back, a plausible argument could be constructed for saying that 1963, the date of Vaizey's book, was the opening of the new era whose apotheosis we shall be describing in this book: the dawning of the realization that curriculum was problematic and needed analysis and public accord, that a pluralistic society shaking off the norms and constraints of class and conformity would send shock waves into the classroom, and that an economy no longer able to rely upon historical pre-eminence and upon colonial cheap raw material and assured markets would create very different public attitudes towards the purposes of education and industrial training. Looking back, we see the 1960s as a social and economic watershed; but we experienced them at the time as a sense of liberation and of the infinite possibilities of new horizons. In the education service, the emphasis was not on how to control but on how to awaken new visions and to encourage the system and teachers we had to rise to them.

Both the Newsom and Robbins Reports were published in 1963, the one about giving an adequate education to half our future, the other about expanding higher education. The Crowther Report about the 15–18 age-group was published four years earlier and the Plowden Report on primary education four years later. The DES set up the Curriculum Study Group in 1962, and that led to the Schools Council in 1964 (after LEAs and teachers had asserted their rights, alongside those of government, over curriculum and examinations). Thus the 1960s saw the arrival of the new in education and tried to capture it within the expansionist, optimistic and consensual spirit of that decade: it made little difference whether the government was Conservative (until 1964) or Labour (until 1970). The essential point is that the structures of control were not challenged or changed: rather the eyes of both politicians and professionals were set on how to realize new objectives; the system – at the deeper level of power relationships – was broadly and unconsciously assumed to be suitable for their achievement. David Eccles's foray into the secret garden of the curriculum, for example, was soon recaptured within the consensus as expressed in the Schools Council. Now we see it as the first move in the government's taking control of the school curriculum. Robbins became a charter for expansion and new thinking in higher education: now we see that expansion and its dependence on public funding as the cause of government control of the universities, in the name of public accountability and economic survival.

The 1960s closed with the publication of the first Black Paper (1969): an accurate augury of the reaction that was to gather strength in the 1970s and find expression in the 1980s. In another sense, the 1960s ended with the White Paper of 1972 entitled *Education: A Framework for Expansion*, the last example this century of a government's feeling able to address education in optimistic financial mood, and all in ruins within a year. By the mid-1970s the anxieties caused by the world oil crisis and hyperinflation, taken with the sterling crisis and a great fear that the British economy had fundamental weaknesses, were finding expression in speeches such as Crosland's 'The party's over' and Callaghan's at Ruskin College, both in 1976. Thereafter, as we shall see, for a few more years the political consensus held and worked on new themes of public involvement in schooling, accountability, education and industry connections, and youth training during a period of mass unemployment and financial retrenchment. Then, after 1986, the radical phase of Conservative policy-making in education asserted simultaneously a massive centralization of power on the one hand and a market economy in schooling on the other.

It is the results of the *dirigisme* since Ruskin, seen in the context of thirty years of change, that we shall examine in this book. The outcome is a scene that would have been unrecognizable to John Vaizey, even though he had transferred his political allegiance from left to right by the time he died. To realize that is to appreciate both how new and how fragile is so much of what we shall describe and what you, as a new teacher, will work among. I hope that in another thirty years someone now relatively new in the service (for so I still think of it) will write the next instalment.

THE ORGANIZATION OF THE BOOK

The book is organized to help you make sense of events and ideas in more or less the order you will encounter them as you move through your education as a teacher and then into schools.

Part 1 is about the initial education and training of teachers. It gives you something of the historical background, so that you can feel a part of the long process by which the education and training of teachers in this country has been improved and given higher status. Then it explains the way in which there is currently something like a 'national curriculum' for teacher training, which should help in understanding the structure and purpose of your own course.

Part 2 is called 'Working in school'. The first two chapters take you from the stage when you are seeking your first post as a teacher, through to induction, and to contracts and conditions of service. Then there are two chapters about the curriculum – your major concern as a teacher. After this we return to matters which impinge upon you personally as an employee as well as a professional: the appraisal of teachers, opportunities for in-service training, and the powers of the school governors.

Part 3 is called 'Trying to make sense of it'. By the time you reach this section, you will know a good deal about *what* has happened, especially in the past twenty years, to change fundamentally the patterns of control over education. Now we try to answer the question of *why* it happened. In Chapter 9, we analyse the way in which the powers and duties of the LEAs have been drastically changed and much reduced. Finally, in Chapter 10, we look at and try to find explanations for the policies of central government since 1979.

The last section of Chapter 10 is a brief but heartfelt message to you yourself as a teacher.

I acknowledge with gratitude the permission of Chapman & Hall to quote from Stuart Maclure's splendid historical source book, *Educational Documents*. Where possible I have used it in preference to the original because it will be more accessible for students. I also acknowledge the kind permission of the Controller of Her Majesty's Stationery Office to quote from or reproduce Crown Copyright material in official documents. My special thanks go to colleagues who have helped me with advice and criticism on various drafts, the series editor Jonathan Solity, George Timmons, Joan Browne and, particularly, Viv

Little. Pauline Porter has retyped and revised each draft stage with great care and enthusiasm. I owe them all a great deal, but the shortcomings remain my own. My final and heartfelt thanks go to my wife, who has forgone my company at weekends while I crammed this writing into a life already over-busy.

John Tomlinson

PART 1

INITIAL TEACHER EDUCATION

CHAPTER 1

The education and training of teachers

The curriculum and the administrative arrangements for the training of teachers were the first things to be taken under tighter central control by the Thatcher governments of the 1980s. This is not generally appreciated – understandably, since nearly ten years after it had first asserted this control in 1983, the government was still vilifying the teacher-training system, blaming it for the perceived ills of education and proposing (in 1992) yet further reform. It was, in fact, the first assertion of a national curriculum and also the first example of such a curriculum not meeting the intentions of those who asserted it.

As you train to become a teacher it will be useful to know something of how the syllabuses and systems you follow are controlled, whence comes their authority, and to what extent your teachers are able to follow their own devices. Such knowledge will be useful in at least two ways. It will help you to understand the origin of the broad structure and content of the course; and it will help you interpret the continuing example it represents of how teachers may work under a national curriculum – as you yourself will be doing in school.

There is also a deeper reason. Just as education reveals society's hopes and intentions for its young, so the spirit in which teachers are trained must be the most sensitive litmus paper of all to indicate how much those in authority really care about the education of the people. It is no accident that in a period of the reassertion of a national curriculum, it happened first in teacher training.

Looking at the hundred years leading up to the 1980s, however, teacher-training policy is revealed as largely the consequence of government policy towards schools, especially policy
concerning the length of compulsory schooling and the content
of the curriculum. The development of teacher-training policy
thus proceeds *post hoc* and in flurries of interest, connected
with prior or concurrent shifts in policy (or aspirations) for the
schools. The Bryce Commission of 1895 thought about
teachers because it was looking at secondary education; the
1925 Departmental Committee on Teacher Training for
Elementary Schools followed the Fisher Act of 1918 (though
Fisher's reforms were largely already doomed because of the
severe cuts in public expenditure known as the Geddes Axe);
the McNair Report of 1944 was consequent upon the thinking
of the Hadow Reports (1926, 1931, 1933) and the 1942 White
Paper on post-war reconstruction. The James Committee of
1971 was set up because of the sea changes in schools brought
about by social change, enlarged curricula, the move to comprehensive secondary education and raising the school leaving
age. Two exceptions to this general analysis then follow: the
reorganization of training colleges in the 1970s and 1980s was
driven mainly by the prospect of falling school rolls, which
required a reduction in the number of teachers in training,
reinforced and shaped by a view that a monotechnic college
culture should be replaced by the 'polytechnic' culture of
'mainstream' higher education institutions. And the reforms of
the late 1980s were largely driven by a political ideology, itself
based in the unproved conviction that establishments of
teacher training were still attached to 'progressive' views on
education, which the government wished to eradicate.

The story is that of a struggle to attract and train teachers of
quality in the numbers and places needed. Intertwined in this
story is another, of the way in which the meaning of what it is
to be a teacher was argued and refined and made both more
generous and more demanding. As we shall see at the end of this
chapter, great successes were achieved; but the future is
problematic.

We can start our brief review of how the British have viewed
teacher training by recalling the report of the Royal Commission on Secondary Education of 1895 (the Bryce Report). Of
teachers it says (Maclure, 1968: 145):

The fact is that the body of teachers must necessarily occupy a
somewhat anomalous position in the economy of national life.

4

The service which they render is one over which the State must in self-defence retain effective oversight; the provision of teaching and the conduct of education cannot be left to private enterprise alone. Nor, on the other hand, do the teachers stand in the same relation to Government as does the Civil Service. Education is a thing too intimately concerned with individual preference and private life, for it to be desirable to throw the whole of it under Government control. It needs organization, but it would be destroyed by uniformity; it is stimulated by inspection, but it could be crushed by a code. In the public service, where the chief object is administrative efficiency, the individual officer is necessarily subordinate; in education, where a chief object is the discovery of more perfect methods of teaching, the individual teacher must be left comparatively free. Every good teacher is a discoverer, and, in order to make discoveries, he must have liberty of experiment.

It is notable that in conceptualizing the ideal teacher the Bryce Report expressed eloquently the paradigm that, during the consensus period of 1945–75, the majority of those concerned for education would advocate for all teachers. In this view the teacher is an active agent, not a passive transmitter of knowledge and skills laid down by others. In Bryce's expression 'every good teacher is a discoverer' there is a foretaste of Stenhouse's 'teacher as researcher'. Let us make no mistake, however: one hundred years ago such a view of the teacher was reserved for those working in secondary schools, and the Bryce Report itself, concerned with secondary education, noted 'the social estrangement between different grades of teachers'.

The first national inquiry instituted this century into the training of teachers was by a departmental committee which looked into the training of teachers for public elementary schools. It was chaired by Lord Burnham and reported in 1925. Its terms of reference were based on the administrative distinction between elementary schools and secondary schools. The report pointed out that this distinction was 'more of an administrative convenience than a desirable educational difference to be perpetuated' (Maclure, 1968: 176). Yet it recommended that university courses, including a degree, should last four years, while training colleges, where there was more concentration on professional training, should have their students for only two years. To try to draw the two sectors more closely together, however, it recommended that responsibility for awarding the teacher's certificate should pass from the Board of Education to joint examination boards of universities and colleges. It may seem surprising that the Board should be willing to accept such a transfer of power. When it is viewed, however, as part of

5

the general willingness to slacken control over curriculum at this period (as we shall see in Chapter 4) and the anxiety then current among some Conservatives that they should not concentrate too much power at the centre, against the day when the first Labour government might be elected, it is less surprising. The change was made in 1928 and joint examination boards were put under the general supervision of the Central Advisory Committee for the Certification of Teachers. The Board of Education, however, retained the right to lay down a minimum period of supervised school practice, which became the basis, in the 1980s and 1990s, of the move towards placing the majority of professional training in the schools.

In 1942, in the midst of the Second World War, as part of its preparation for post-war reconstruction, the government appointed a committee chaired by Sir Arnold McNair, Vice-Chancellor of Liverpool University, to investigate the supply, recruitment and training of teachers. In the autumn of 1942, R.A. Butler addressed the annual conference of the Training Colleges Association, and 'described himself as one of the few Presidents of the Board in recent times who had a keen enough interest in the training of teachers to want to have a thorough enquiry into it' (Browne, 1979: 52). There had been advocacy for some years among the training college staffs for a three-year course and improved material conditions in colleges, with more generous staffing and opportunities for research 'so that colleges could provide the civilising influence and academic stimulus that the universities could offer their students' (Browne, 1979: 51). With that background, and with the intention that the new Education Act (1944) should propose an end to elementary schools and offer 'secondary education for all', the McNair Committee worked in a context where a radical shake-up and improvement in the recruitment and training of teachers were expected.

The McNair Report of 1944 recommended that the course of training should last three years from age 18, followed by a year's probation after qualification. It stated (Maclure, 1968: 216) that:

> Three things in particular must be done if the number and quality of teachers required to match the reforms proposed in the White Paper are to be obtained. The field of recruitment must be widened; conditions of service which deter people from becoming teachers must be abolished; and the standing of education must be improved so that a sufficient number of men and women of quality will be attracted to teaching as a profession.

The government accepted the idea of a three-year course, removed the ban on married women teachers, set up area training organizations linking colleges and universities, and created the National Advisory Council for the Training and Supply of Teachers as a standing advisory body. The report also recommended higher salaries, and these were indeed negotiated in the Burnham Committee in 1947.

The report was hailed as a teachers' charter, but in some respects it raised expectations that have still not been realized. In particular, scant attention was paid to the principles of professional status recommended in the report, and they remain a matter of unfinished business in the 1990s, as the arguments about whether to create a general teaching council demonstrate. However, government action following the McNair Report created the framework for teacher training until the changes of the 1970s. There remained the distinction between the one-year postgraduate certificate in education taken after a university degree, and the college course of higher education concurrent with professional training, but at least the need for the three-year course had been accepted (it was actually implemented in 1960). None the less, a university graduate could still be recognized as a qualified teacher without undertaking any postgraduate training (that route was not removed until the 1970s). In advocating the joint boards of colleges and universities (not to be confused with the joint examining boards mentioned earlier), the Report emphasized the Committee's view that closer contact between colleges and universities would be advantageous (Maclure, 1968: 220):

> provided that it takes the form of a partnership between equals and does not lead to the universities having a predominant influence in the training of students in the training colleges . . . in each area the university and every training college should become conscious that they are all engaged, each in its different way, in the common task of training teachers . . . for the purpose of a more unified service.

The post-war period was thus one in which the education service was increasingly seen as a unified whole – as, indeed, a public service working alongside other services for the amelioration of society; and underpinning this was a sense that the distinctions between teachers in different stages of education and kinds of school were inappropriate. Successive Burnham Reports on salaries and conditions of service moved to reduce these distinctions, as did the philosophies of both primary and secondary education, and this therefore also became the predominant culture of those working in teacher education and training, in both colleges and universities.

The decade 1960–70 was one of the most hectic ever experienced by colleges and departments of education. The three-year course was introduced in the colleges in 1960, informed by a sense that standards needed to rise as school curricula changed. To meet a rapidly rising school population, the number of teachers in training was increased from 60,000 in 1961–2 to 120,000 in 1971–2; all kinds of expedient to intensify the use of buildings and staff were pressed into service – 'Cox-and-Box', 'the extended college year' and 'home and away' came into the vocabulary. By the end of the decade, attention had turned from the urgent need to increase supply to the content, structure and organization of training. In 1969, a select committee of the House of Commons began a major study of teacher training, and the following year the area training organizations (ATOs) – that is, the groupings of university and colleges set up following McNair – were asked by the Secretary of State to review their courses and procedures. These moves set the stage for the next major governmental inquiry into teacher training. Towards the end of 1970, Edward Short, the Secretary of State, appointed a committee under the chairmanship of Lord James, Vice-Chancellor of the University of York. They had available the evidence brought together by the Select Committee and the ATO enquiry. They were asked to work quickly and completed their report within a year. It was published in January 1972, by which time Margaret Thatcher had become Secretary of State.

The James Report was notable for its attempt to look at the training needed by a teacher over a lifetime's work. It also advocated an all-graduate profession, and an education and training system that was 'wholeheartedly' accepted into 'the family of higher education institutions'.

As we shall see in Chapter 7, the government accepted the James Committee's recommendation of a fourfold increase in in-service training, to 3 per cent of the teaching force being involved annually (although deterioration in the economy prevented the target ever being reached). The government also accepted the principle that the induction/probationary year should be seen as very important to the new teacher and better provided for. The prospects of raising the school leaving age (1972–3) and the already heavy reliance of schools upon probationary teachers made rapid movement towards better induction impossible. The argument still continues in the 1990s. On the core issue of initial education and training, the

James Committee's proposals proved controversial, and in the end government policy developed more as a result of other pressures and imperatives. The aim of an all-graduate profession was, however, accepted as 'the ultimate aim' (DES, 1972b: para. 73). In effect, from the argument following James, there emerged the three- and four-year degrees (ordinary and honours), which combine training and education and which became the dominant form of training for most primary-school teachers and many in secondary schools for at least two decades. Alongside that route, those who first graduated in a 'subject degree' continued to be trained through the post-graduate certificate in education (PGCE).

The argument that followed James's recommendations forced the government to state their own principles concerning the organization and administration of teacher training. This was done in the White Paper of 1972, *Education: A Framework for Expansion* (DES, 1972b). I quote it at length here because it stands for the last occasion on which a government acknowledged the principles of academic freedom, professional involvement and government policy as each having independent status, and the desirability of bringing them into useful interaction to support the training of teachers. The thrust of government policy in the 1980s was, in the spirit of those times, directive and instrumental, with government predominant. Here are some paragraphs from *Education: A Framework for Expansion* which should be read in that context: a last flare in the search for consensus, which was abandoned in teacher training earlier than for the service generally (DES, 1972b: 26–8):

89. It is important to distinguish the main functions that need to be discharged in relation to teacher training. In the Government's view these concern, respectively: academic validation, professional recognition, co-ordination, and higher education supply.

90. Academic validation is here taken to mean determining whether the conditions of entry to and the structure of courses, including school and other practical experience, the content and level of syllabuses and the standard of achievement required, justify the award of a certificate, diploma or degree. In the Government's view this function should remain the responsibility of existing academic bodies – the senates of universities, the academic boards of polytechnics and colleges of education and the Council for National Academic Awards (C.N.A.A.).

91. The Government expect, however, that these bodies will continue and, indeed, develop the arrangements by which the teaching profession and the local education authorities are

associated closely with their work. Some colleges, singly or jointly with others as at present, may seek academic awards from a university, others from the C.N.A.A.

92. The function of professional recognition is to determine, first, whether the professional content, structure and standards of courses are such as to warrant the acceptance as qualified teachers of students who complete them satisfactorily; secondly, whether candidates for admission to the profession are acceptable on other than academic grounds; and thirdly, whether new entrants may be judged to have completed their probation satisfactorily and to be eligible for registration. The Government think it right that in the teaching profession, as in others, members of the profession should have a major, though not exclusive, role in the discharge of this function; and that in this context teachers in colleges and departments of education should be regarded, as they regard themselves, as members of the teaching profession no less than those who work in schools. Future arrangements should reflect this general principle.

93. The third function includes the promotion, co-ordination and supervision of in-service training, an improved system of induction, and the professional centres related to both; of the allocation of teaching practice; and of the distribution of teacher training courses, in number and kind, among higher education institutions.

94. By the fourth function, higher education supply, is meant the development, financial support and control of higher education institutions. The Government recognise that improved arrangements are required for planning and co-ordination in the non-university sector . . . In the meantime responsibility for this function, both generally and in relation to teacher training, will continue to rest where it does now.

95. It is in respect of the third function that the Government share the view of the James Committee that new regional machinery is required. Effective co-ordination needs the close co-operation of the local education authorities, the training institutions and their staff, and the teaching profession. The Government therefore propose that after further consultation the Secretary of State should establish, in place of the existing university-based A.T.O.s, new regional committees to co-ordinate the education and training of teachers, composed in such a way as properly to reflect these three sets of interests. These committees will not have executive or financial responsibility for the services they co-ordinate; this will remain with the local education authorities and the training agencies who will need to include in their estimates suitable provision for in-service training. The administrative costs of the committees will be met by direct grant from the Department.

96. The demarcation of suitable regions for this purpose presents serious difficulties which cannot be resolved until firmer decisions can be reached on the fourth function identified above - supply. Meanwhile the Secretary of State hopes that the A.T.O.s will

continue to discharge their existing responsibilities for both initial and in-service training.

97. There remains the question by what machinery the Secretary of State can best obtain the advice of the local authorities and other providing bodies, the teaching profession and the institutions themselves, on the discharge of her central responsibilities for teacher supply and training. The Government accept the recommendation on this matter of the Working Party which reported in 1970 [on a teaching council for England and Wales] and the Secretary of State has it in mind after consultation to establish an Advisory Committee on the Supply and Training of Teachers broadly on the model then recommended.

98. The Government also agree with the report of the Working Party that a separate body is required to concern itself with the professional recognition functions referred to above. There is, however, no alternative to responsibility for professional recognition continuing to rest with the Secretary of State unless the outcome of any further discussions justifies her in deciding to share this responsibility with a Teaching Council set up on the lines recommended in the report. The Government are anxious, however, that in the meantime there should be arrangements for advising the Secretary of State on the discharge of this responsibility which would recognise the general principle that the profession should have a major but not exclusive voice. The Government propose to consult further with the interests concerned – the teachers, their employers and the institutions in which teachers are educated and trained – as to how this might best be effected.

In the event, the driving organizational principles for teacher training during the 1970s were rationalization, the establishment of direct arrangements for accreditation and validation by the colleges with either a university or the Council for National Academic Awards (CNAA), and movement from a monotechnic to a polytechnic culture. Many small colleges closed; many others combined with a polytechnic or university. A few monotechnic colleges survived, mainly in the denominational sector, and some still exist. In 1970, there were 27 universities and 180 colleges producing 40,000 new teachers a year. By the early 1980s, there were 27 universities and 84 colleges/polytechnics producing only 17,000 teachers a year. The reduction was imposed almost entirely upon the three- and four-year courses, which fell from nearly 40,000 admissions each year in the early 1970s to under 10,000 in 1982, while the PGCE course admissions remained more or less constant (Figure 1.1).

Nearly all these changes were the result of government decisions from 1977 onwards. By the early 1980s, a sea change

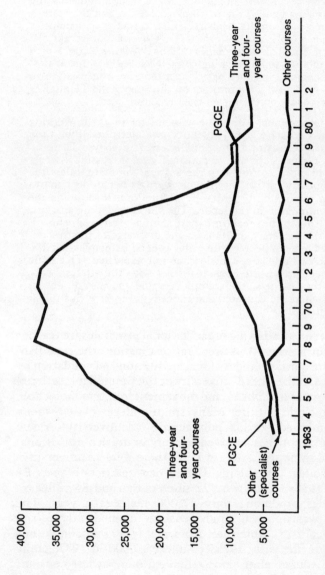

**Figure 1.1 Students admitted to courses of initial teacher training in England and Wales 1963–1982.
Source: Alexander (1984: 104), quoted in Furlong et al. (1988: 3).**

had occurred overall. The colleges had for the most part become departments or faculties in multipurpose polytechnics or universities, and the bruising experiences of closure, redeployment of staff, large-scale early retirement of other staff and adjustment to new institutional cultures, not least the emphasis in universities upon research, had transformed the initial teacher-training scene.

Most of the remaining staff reacted swiftly and positively to the excitement and stimulus of this enlarged culture, which could only, in the long view, be beneficial to the intellectual development of teachers and their professional status. Regrettably, the changes occurred in a period of retrenchment and had not everywhere taken root before the next wave of change arrived.

It was thus upon this still unsettled and immature system that the new imperatives of the Conservative government of the early 1980s began to bear. In the search to 'raise standards', the government by 1983 had turned its attention to 'teaching quality'. The White Paper of that title published in March that year devoted half of its hundred paragraphs to the initial training of teachers. Sections 3, 4 and 5 were entitled 'The match between the teacher's training and his work', 'Initial teacher training – the structure of provision' and 'The content of initial training and the qualification of teachers' (DES, 1983).

Teaching Quality proposed the fundamental change that, in future, teacher-training courses should be approved by the Secretary of State after being judged against a single set of national criteria, instead of the decision being based on the recommendations of the local college/university professional committees. 'Approval' in this sense means whether the course as a whole may be recognized as conferring qualified teacher status: it is separate from the academic validation of the course, once approved. Although it was revolutionary and *dirigiste* in character, the proposal did not evoke general hostility, and teacher trainers themselves saw the advantage of clarity of purpose being externally set rather than continuing to be an issue of contention between government, the profession and the training institutions. Moreover, there had been discussion and consultation through the Advisory Committee on the Supply and Education of Teachers (ACSET). The Committee had offered preliminary advice in January 1983 (which is printed in full as Annex B to *Teaching Quality*) and stood ready to offer further advice, subject to the government's wishes.

The key paragraph of *Teaching Quality* is number 63 (DES, 1983):

> 63. The Secretaries of State propose to promulgate criteria, drawn up in consultation with the appropriate professional and academic bodies through A.C.S.E.T. against which they will in future assess initial training courses before deciding whether to approve them. These criteria will relate to both professional and academic content of courses, and to good working relationships with schools. They will provide a framework within which training institutions and professional committees will be able to plan and scrutinize courses before submitting them to the Secretaries of State for approval. The Secretaries of State propose to re-establish the professional committees with fresh guidelines and with constitutions to be approved by them. In approving courses they will not seek to duplicate the work of the institutions and committees, but rather to satisfy themselves that individual course proposals are consistent with the published criteria. Once the criteria are published, the Secretaries of State will initiate a review of all existing approved courses of initial training. They may withdraw approval from those courses which do not conform to the criteria.

The criteria were to impose three broad requirements:

1 at least two years' subject study at higher education level;
2 adequate attention to teaching method;
3 studies closely linked with practical experience in school, and involving the active participation of experienced, practising school teachers.

The detailed criteria and procedures were subsequently laid down in DES Circular no. 3/84, 13 April 1984 (DES, 1984). Others were added in Teacher Training Circular Letter 7/84 in October 1984, following further advice from ACSET. The whole system was to be focused upon and administered by a new national body, the Council for the Accreditation of Teacher Education (CATE). The criteria would be laid down by the Secretary of State, but scrutiny of courses and advice on whether to recognize them or not would go to the Secretary of State from CATE. In June 1985, CATE issued a digest of the criteria (CATE, 1985). It tried to present in tabulated form the 2,000 words of text, 'Criteria for the approval of courses', contained in the annex to Circular 3/84. The headings were:

1 selection of students (15 points to be observed);
2 staff (3 points);
3 course organization (4 points);
4 subject studies and subject method (8 points);

5   educational and professional studies (12 points);
6   student assessment and certification (3 points).

The considerable task of scrutinizing a variety of courses (four-year degree, three-year degree, shortened two-year degree in shortage subjects, PGCE; and all separated as between intending infants, junior and secondary teachers) in more than ninety institutions took five years in the first place. HMI visited and reported upon the institution; then the institution prepared its submission to CATE; then CATE met representatives of the institution, and often set in hand further enquiries or arranged visits before deciding upon a recommendation. The Secretary of State then considered the recommendation and finally gave approval, withheld approval or gave only temporary approval.

Whatever the merits of the theory of national scrutiny against agreed criteria, the practice in the first phase (1985–89) attracted criticism in several respects. The criteria, as applied in the bureaucracy of CATE, led to consideration of the minutiae of course content, course organization, contacts with schools, staff qualifications and student selection or prior qualification. There was, therefore, a good deal of professional dissatisfaction not with the principle but with the practice. It also meant that teacher training was seen as a different species of study, especially in universities, subject to external controls of an invasive kind.

At the same time, during the late 1980s and early 1990s a critique of teacher training was becoming increasingly vocal from the radical new right, who found a receptive ear in some parts of government during the third Thatcher administration and then during John Major's. At its most extreme, this view would have abolished formal initial teacher training altogether and replaced it with an 'apprenticeship' system based in the schools. Such an approach had worked, it was argued, for many untrained graduates in the independent and former grammar schools, and also had the virtue of exposing the teacher immediately to 'reality', while avoiding the dangers of exposure to learning theory or any of the disciplines connected with an understanding of child development and the social influences upon child, family and school.

There had been some respectable research into the questions of the balance between school-based and college-based components of initial training courses, and of the most effective structures for pursuing the school-based element and gaining maximum benefit from it. In 1983, the DES had commissioned a major research study, the results of which were published in 1988 as *Initial Teacher Training and the Role of the School* (Furlong *et al.*, 1988). The research distinguished four levels or forms of teacher training:

1 direct practice: in the classroom;
2 indirect practice: practical training in classes and workshops within the institution;
3 practical principles: critical study of the principles of practice and their use;
4 disciplinary theory: critical study of practice in the light of theory and research.

The object of the levels of training was to provide an ability to be reflective about practice which 'requires that students be introduced in a developmental way to the complexities of teaching situations' (Furlong *et al.*, 1988: 207). The courses of training researched showed that there had been considerable movement away from any simple dichotomy of 'theory' and 'practice'. The development of a larger component of school-based training and a better understanding, in both schools and institutions, of its uses could be seen as a progressive rejection of the traditional model, in which training began with a 'detached' understanding of how to practise in school, which was then 'applied'. Such a development asserted that professional practice is best understood and developed through 'reflection in action' rather than as 'application of theory'. It was found, moreover, that students trained in this way handled unfamiliar or difficult situations well as probationary teachers.

The research also made it clear that to achieve a fruitful balance of school-based and institution-based training certain conditions had to be present:

• Preparation is needed not only for the work in school, but also for the range of professional activities in and out of school.
• Practising teachers who take responsibility for school-based work need extra time and in-service training.
• Alternative examples of good practice to that seen in the school should be provided by the institution.
• To develop a critical approach to their own practice, students need to be introduced to analysis of the professional practice of the teachers they work with in school.

The teachers themselves therefore need to be able to undertake and share such critical reflection.
• The work at level 4 can only be done adequately by the institutions.

There was no national forum in which such research findings could be discussed and so contribute to the development of government policy, because ACSET had been abolished and nothing put in its place. Experiments born of the apprenticeship view went ahead with 'licensed teachers' and 'articled teachers' in a pragmatic way.

At the same time, the National Council for Vocational Qualifications (NCVQ) was basing its approach to the accreditation of courses almost entirely upon 'outcome criteria'. At first this did not seem to affect teacher training. In 1990, CATE was reconstituted with a wider remit. In future it was not only to scrutinize courses for the purpose of accreditation but also to monitor them to see if there had been 'slippage', identify and disseminate good practice, keep the criteria under review, and give advice to the Secretary of State. In other words, some of the functions of ACSET were revived and given to CATE. The revised criteria were set out in DES Circular no. 24, 10 November 1989 (DES, 1989c). They addressed the same broad spectrum and continued to be detailed and specific as to course content. There were seventy-five different conditions or criteria which had to be applied by institutions, and their complexity was such that it required a ten-page commentary for their explication.

The process of looking once again at over 300 courses had only just begun when the government published a consultation document in January 1992, which proposed further radical reform. As explained in the subsequent Circular no. 9/92, 25 June 1992, three main principles were now to apply (DFE, 1992c: para. 2):

i) schools should play a much larger part in ITT [initial teacher training] as full partners of higher education institutions (HEIs);
ii) the accreditation criteria for ITT courses should require HEIs, schools and students to focus on the competences of teaching; and
iii) institutions, rather than individual courses, should be accredited for ITT.

The initial training courses of the mid-1990s will therefore be, yet again, in a process of transition. There will be many questions, procedures and meanings to be set in place. The notion of 'competences' is akin to outcome criteria rather than to the process criteria used from 1984. Yet some control of process will remain; and the question of what evidence will be required to judge or prove competence will need resolution. There will be a political and financial dimension introduced into the relationships between schools and the institutions, as ambiguous phrases such as 'full partners' are translated into power over course construction and resources. At the time of writing, the proposal is that the institutions retain the responsibility for certifying success or failure in the course and must therefore find ways of satisfying themselves as to quality of content, process and outcome in both school and institution. They will be judged accordingly by Her Majesty's Inspectorate (HMI), CATE and DFE. The notion of accrediting an institution, rather than individual courses, on the basis of a five-year development plan ought to introduce the opportunity for flexibility and experiment which have been almost totally stifled since 1984. But it will depend on how the criteria are interpreted. Crucially, the ability and willingness of schools to work in a contractual relationship with higher education institutions (HEIs), and the ability of the HEIs to finance such contracts and maintain quality with funds which will not be increased, must raise serious anxieties.

In sum, therefore, and in advance of knowing the government's proposals for primary-teacher training, it looks as though the training course you will experience will be in transition, at least until the mid-1990s and in some cases until the end of the decade. Most four-year courses will not begin to apply the new criteria until 1995. But, though changing, they will remain unquestionably under the control of central government in most essential respects.

TEACHER TRAINING: RETROSPECT AND PROSPECTS

The story of teacher training this century can be seen as a continual struggle to attract and train teachers of quality. On this view, those engaged in that struggle gained success after success, as the level of education required and the length and quality of training were raised progressively until both graduate status and training were required of all who became teachers. In that story certain landmarks stand out: McNair's recom-

The education and training of teachers: landmarks

1895   The Bryce Committee Report (secondary)

1925   Departmental committee on teacher training for elementary schools – chaired by Lord Burnham

1928   Joint examination boards of universities and colleges for teacher training (replacing the Board of Education)

1944   The McNair Report: three-year course recommended; setting up of the National Advisory Council for the Training and Supply of Teachers, and the area training organizations (ATOs) (universities and colleges)

1960   Three-year course replaces two-year course

1960s   Rapid expansion: from 60,000 teachers in training (1963) to 120,000 (1970)

1969   House of Commons Select Committee studies teacher training

1970s   Rapid contraction: from 120,000 in training to 40,000; graduate training a requirement; diversification – the end of single-purpose colleges

1970   ATOs asked to review their courses and James Committee appointed

1972   James Report; *Education: A Framework for Expansion* – White Paper

1983   *Teaching Quality* – White Paper; national criteria proposed; Council for the Accreditation of Teacher Education (CATE) proposed

1984   DES Circular no. 3/84 and Teacher Training Letter no. 7/84 (the new criteria)

1985–9   First scrutiny by CATE of colleges and universities; licensed and articled teacher-training schemes introduced by DES

1989   Revised criteria – DES Circular no. 24/89

1992   Secretary of State calls for more school-based work in training courses; DFE Circular no. 9/92 and CATE Notes for Guidance on secondary courses; proposals for primary-teacher education awaited

1989–   Campaign by organizations of teachers, LEAs, governors, parents, the churches and higher education for a statutory general teaching council; still at work

mendation of the three-year course, its achievement in 1960, the introduction of the BEd honours degree, the requirement for all graduates to be trained, and the bringing of teacher training into the main stream of higher education.

Seen from a rather different standpoint, that of asking what was put under control and why, a clear and positive judgement is more difficult to make. The extreme forms of the ideology which advocates total school-based, apprenticeship-style training or excessive proportions of it in training courses, and some of the expedients used to increase teacher supply during the crisis of the late 1980s, betoken an impoverished or dismissive view of the importance of professional training adequately grounded in critical reflection and academic discipline. Furthermore, the emphasis that has been placed on using in-service education and training (INSET) to train narrowly so as to teach the National Curriculum, and the risk of overemphasizing the schools' national curriculum in the higher education of teacher-training students, suggest both an 'operative' view of the teacher and an instrumental view of higher education. Again, as in so much else we shall examine in this book, the question may come to turn on which aspect of new right thinking comes to predominate. If it is the central control of National Curriculum as the entitlement of pupils and therefore requiring a highly educated and trained body of teachers, then the struggle for quality may register further successes. But if the market is allowed to predominate and school governors, ultimately, may employ whom they wish and can afford, then any kind of systematic development of quality will recede as an aim of policy. It is upon this hinge, perhaps more than any other, that the decision of government whether to create a general teaching council, and thereby introduce into the profession an element of self-regulation and a watchdog of the public interest, will turn.

NOTE ON A GENERAL TEACHING COUNCIL

A general teaching council would regulate standards in the profession of teaching and would be comparable to the General Medical Council or the council which regulates the nursing profession. It would be concerned with the whole profession, covering schools and further and higher education, and would be composed of both teachers and lay people. Its overriding purpose would be to maintain and, over time, raise standards in both the professional and the public interest.

It is surprising that teachers remain virtually the only considerable grouping that has not achieved a measure of self-regulation. Entry to and exit from the profession, together with control over the standards of entry training, are all in the hands of the Secretary of State. Legislation was introduced in 1901, but not followed up. In 1970, a DES Committee (Weaver) suggested ways forward, and in 1990 the House of Commons Select Committee for Education, Science and Arts (ESAC) recommended the creation of a general teaching council (GTC).

Meanwhile the profession has, for the first time, united in an effort to promote the creation of such a council. More than thirty national organizations, including not only all the teachers' associations but also local authorities, governors, parents and the churches, have created a national forum and have set up an organization to promote a statutory GTC. That group published in July 1992 *Proposals for a Statutory General Teaching Council for England and Wales* (GTC, 1992b), which sets out in detail the case for a GTC and draft legislation (available from GTC (England & Wales), 27 Britannia Street, London WC1X 9JP).

The government remains opposed to a GTC, presumably because it does not wish to surrender the control over the profession which the current arrangements give it.

PART 2

WORKING IN SCHOOL

CHAPTER 2

Your first post in teaching: probation and induction

YOUR FIRST POST: HOW WILL YOU GET IT? WHAT WILL BE EXPECTED OF YOU?

Your experience in your first post will be very important to you, not only for its effect at the time but also for the way it shapes your future career – through both what you do and so become and the judgement others make of you. It is therefore worth thinking about the systems of control that will be acting upon you as you go through the process of seeking your first job and then coming to terms with it. The conventions and regulations governing appointment procedures, contracts of employment and the practical details of a teacher's working schedule are essentially the same for all teachers: but for the new teacher, experiencing them personally for the first time, they assume special significance, and it is as well to have some idea of what to expect and what will be expected of you.

There are about 25,000 schools in Great Britain, and since the 1988 Education Reform Act the governing body of each school has been the authority which selects, appoints and dismisses teachers. In county schools the LEA is the employer in law; in aided and grant-maintained schools, city technology colleges and independent schools, the governors are also the employer. The first thing to appreciate, therefore, is that when seeking and getting your first post (or any post for that matter), each job application procedure is almost certainly going to be a particular and different experience. Procedures can be broadly described and are similar in essentials everywhere: but the way in which individual LEAs, governing bodies and schools apply them, the degree of formality or informality, the opportunity given or not given to visit the school and meet the teachers who may be your future colleagues in circumstances that encourage a truthful exchange of ideas – all these and much more of the important subtext are determined by the particular individuals controlling the system. The best advice to the new teacher seeking a first post is to be yourself, seize opportunities (whether intended or not) to look behind the façade, and use your own judgement about the quality of the people and processes you encounter, while accepting that you must conform to whatever system of appointment is being used – if you want to stay in with a chance of getting the job.

The most reliable source of evidence of the experience of 'new teachers' is two surveys conducted by HMI, in 1981 and 1987. Each led to the publication of a document entitled *The New Teacher in School* (DES, 1982, 1988b). As we shall see, they provide very useful information and insight. But they antedate the introduction of the National Curriculum and assessment, and all the other changes following from the 1988 Education Reform Act. As I write, the HMI report on the induction and probation of new teachers (DES, 1992b) has been published, and we shall use information from that in considering the induction of new teachers.

THE PROCESS OF APPOINTMENT

If the schools in one LEA need a large number of teachers in a particular year, then they and the LEA may decide to co-operate to create a pool. When appointments were made by LEAs and teachers were in short supply, this was a common and efficient way of making first appointments. The candidates did not have to make multiple applications and attend numerous interviews, and the schools did not have to deploy so many staff in interview panels. In the circumstances of the 1990s, pools are much rarer, though still used in some LEAs, especially in urban areas. If you seek and gain appointment to a pool, remember that while it secures you employment, you will still have to gain the approval of the governors and head of an individual school. That might involve further interviews, depending on the procedure used in the area.

Whether it is via a pool or directly to a school, the appointment process must begin by finding that a job is available.

This is usually done through national advertisement, but some LEAs or districts in large LEAs circulate vacancy lists. If for some reason the geographical area of your choice is limited, it will be useful to find out whether such lists are compiled or whether jobs are advertised in the local press. The third source of information is often the school(s) in which the classroom experience elements of the initial training course are based.

Advertisements need interpretation. The words used to describe the tasks to be performed will have meant something particular to those who drafted them; and there are many varieties and size of school within the broad categories of primary, middle or secondary. The variety of schools is illustrated by the information HMI collected in 1987 about the schools to which the 297 teachers in their survey were appointed (Figure 2.1). These data reveal six or seven different sizes of primary and secondary school; twelve different designations of school age-range and purpose; and five or seven kinds of social and geographical setting. Even in the 1990s, when educational reforms have introduced so much national control and convergence into the system, the real-life situations of the schools themselves remain doggedly individual. In seeking your first post you should not only be acutely aware of this, but also welcome it as offering an opportunity, if you are skilful enough, to find a placement where you can be really effective.

So, advertisements need interpretation. Your university or college department may offer a service of help with this and other aspects of putting together an application. Application forms vary from LEA to LEA and school to school (efforts to get agreement to a 'uniform form' have regrettably always failed – mainly because of the point already made, that those making appointments are jealous of their individuality). Fill in the application form clearly so that the information comes easily off the page to the reader. And always pay special attention to the section 'reasons for applying', 'letter of application' or 'further personal statement'; or if there is none, write your own personal letter of application. It is through this that the reader hears your unique voice. It is the single most important determinant of whether you will be called for interview, assuming you have the basic qualifications required. Something has got to make the reader decide to put you on the short list. Help him or her.

It is also worth spending time compiling a curriculum vitae (CV) – even if you are young rather than a mature entrant and

The schools

1. The distribution of schools by size and phase was as follows:

Table 30 *School size*

Size of school	Number of schools	
	Primary, including	
less than 50 pupils	1	–
50–99	9	–
100–199	29	–
200–399	71	5
400–599	8	15
600–799	2	38
800–999	–	57
1000–1199	–	29
1200–1499	–	24
1500 or more	–	9
	Total 120 schools	**Total 177 schools**

2. The types of schools in which the probationers were employed are shown in the following table:

Table 31 *School type*

Number			
Nursery	1	Middle deemed secondary	7
Infant/First	30	Comprehensive	153
Junior	23	Grammar	8
Junior/Infant	50	Secondary modern	8
Middle deemed primary	5	Sixth form college	7
First and middle	4	Other secondary	1
		Total	**297**

3. Shows the types of catchment area of the schools in the survey. In over a fifth of the primary and middle schools and in 6 per cent of secondary, 20 per cent or more of the children came from homes where English was not the first language.

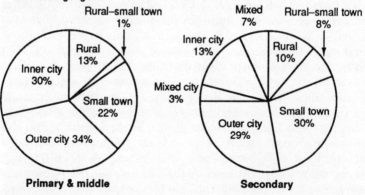

Primary & middle

Secondary

Figure 2.1 Schools to which teachers were appointed, 1987.
Source: DES (1988b: 69–70). Reproduced by permission of the Controller of Her Majesty's Stationery Office.

28

it therefore seems sadly brief! The same ground rules apply as to the application form: it should be easy to read and deftly build a picture of your qualifications, experience, interests and personality. All higher education institutions will offer help with CVs. It is better to get the job done well before you become involved in the hurly-burly of applications and interviews. In both the CV and the application form, use the word-processor skills you will have acquired from your teacher-training course. But, if you write a letter, do so in your own hand: it conveys an important individuality which matters to the discerning selector. It also, very practically, suggests whether the pupils will be able to read what you will write for them!

Do not allow yourself to become dispirited if applications, or even interviews, do not quickly lead to an appointment. Every experience should make you a better candidate, if you make proper use of it. With schools and governors being as various and individual as has been described, it is bound to take time. HMI reported in 1988 that 68 per cent of new teachers had made up to five applications, 19 per cent between six and ten, and 13 per cent more than ten. And that was before the 1988 Education Reform Act put the appointment firmly in the hands of the governing body of each school.

TYPES OF CONTRACT

In Chapter 3, you can read a formal description of the kinds of contract teachers may work under and aspects of the law of employment that surround and support them. Here it should be noted that in 1988 HMI reported that 98 per cent of probationers were on full-time contracts. However, not all of these, even then, were permanent contracts: 18 per cent had been appointed on short-term contracts, usually for one year, but sometimes only for one or two terms. One teacher worked in two different schools during his or her first year, and two secondary probationers were employed as supply teachers – that is, being used to fill in for teacher absences at a variety of schools. Since the introduction of delegated financial management, short-term contracts have become more prevalent as governors have realized that their budgets, which are cash limited, will vary from year to year and that they may therefore have to reduce the number of teachers employed at short notice. In 1992 HMI reported that 'There is a disturbing increase in the numbers of new teachers who are appointed to temporary posts, many of which are of doubtful suitability for probationers' (DES, 1992b: para. 16).

No one with any experience of teaching would recommend employing a new teacher on a short-term contract, because it only adds to the unavoidable strain connected with finding your feet in a new job. However, you should be vigilant about the terms of service that are being offered. If a short-term contract is all that is available, it becomes even more important to negotiate decent induction conditions before accepting, because once employed you will be in a relatively weak position. Moreover, now probation has been abolished, you will have only the general law of employment to protect you.

AFTER APPOINTMENT

Let us now suppose you have gained an appointment at a school. What might you expect to happen before taking up the post, assuming there is a reasonable period of time available? Your wish will be to find out as much as possible of what will be expected of you, to meet those you will be working closely with, and see the conditions in the classroom(s) and the resources available. HMI looked into these issues in their 1987 survey, and their Table 19 summarizes their findings. It

Table 19 Practice prior to the probationers taking up their appointments

Prior to taking up appointments newly trained teachers normally:	Primary & middle %	Secondary %
visit school for information	100	99
visit school to meet staff	100	99
visit school to meet pupils	93	35
visit school to undertake teaching	30	7
receive school handbook	82	90
receive timetable	61	99
receive syllabuses/schemes of work	91	99
receive information on resources	88	94
participate in other arrangements	36	48

Source: DES (1988b: 52)

suggests a very encouraging picture. Virtually all new teachers visited the school, met staff and pupils and got useful information. Moreover, senior staff in the schools thought that these meetings prior to taking up appointment were important, and the new teachers themselves found them of value. However, the table also shows that the practice of schools is not uniform. If you should not be offered a visit and/or information, press for it. The earlier you know about timetable, syllabuses, the classes you will teach and the resources available, the better you will be able to prepare yourself. Control may formally lie in one quarter, but you can transfer some of it to yourself, if you see the need and act in time.

PROBATION AND INDUCTION

We now move into an area of regulation which, at the time of writing, is undergoing radical change. In 1991, the Secretary of State announced that he intended to do away with the requirement that newly trained and appointed teachers should serve a period of probation. For many years, a new teacher appointed to a full-time post had had to serve one year as a probationer. The teacher did not receive full qualified teacher status until probation had been satisfactorily completed. It was the duty of the LEA in a county school to decide whether a positive recommendation should be made.

Although the formal requirement for a period of probation was abolished from September 1992, it is worth recording the guidance formerly given to LEAs and governors by the DES concerning the way in which the new teacher ought to be treated, because it reveals the philosophy which it has been thought should inform the relationship between the new teacher, the school and the LEA or governing body. Much of this has been carried forward into the new requirements surrounding induction, with the significant difference that the regulations for teacher appraisal and the terms of employment law will apply. That represents a fundamentally different relationship between teachers and school: whereas probation could, if necessary, be attempted in more than one school, we do not know how much flexibility will be possible in future. Moreover, whereas since 1989 failure of the probationary year could be redeemed by successful service subsequently in another school (before 1989 failure had meant the end of the teacher's career in the maintained sector), under the new

31

arrangements it will be for a different governing body to decide whether to take on the new teacher whose contract at his or her first school has been cancelled.

Here then are extracts from DES Administrative memorandum no. 1/90, dated 20 April 1990 (only seventeen months before the Secretary of State's letter of 17 September 1991 announcing his proposal to abolish probation). It is called 'The treatment and assessment of probationary teachers' (DES, 1990: 3–7):

SUITABLE APPOINTMENTS FOR PROBATIONERS

11. a. LEAs, or governing bodies as appropriate (including governing bodies of schools with delegated budgets), should as far as possible avoid appointing probationers to short term posts in which they will not be able to serve their full probation period . . . Where appointment to such a post is proposed the LEA or governing body, as appropriate, should ensure that the candidate is aware that:

    (i) if he or she subsequently obtains another appointment there is no entitlement to aggregate the periods of service for probation purposes (unless the periods are both with a single LEA and there is no break between them); and

    (ii) there is no guarantee that probation will be waived or reduced in consequence of the previous appointment.

b. The duties assigned to probationers, their supervision, and the conditions under which they work should be such as to enable a fair and reasonable assessment to be made of their conduct and efficiency as teachers. Probationers should not normally be appointed to posts where they cannot complete probation under acceptable working conditions.

c. Probationers should be given an opportunity to demonstrate their proficiency in teaching classes of a size normal for the school in which they teach and the subject they are teaching.

d. The appointment of newly qualified teachers as supply teachers should be avoided. Where such appointments are inescapable, however, it is essential that the teacher is given appropriate support. Particular care should be taken to ensure that a regular timetable is allotted.

e. Peripatetic appointments are generally unsuitable for newly qualified teachers because they do not provide a stable setting within which the teacher can develop and consolidate his or her skills.

f. New teachers should serve their probation in posts which are closely related to the age group and subjects for which they have been trained. This information is specified on the letters granting qualified teacher status to those successfully completing courses of initial teacher training or a period as a licensed teacher. Their assignments should also take account of their experience. New teachers should not normally serve probation in schools which present unusual problems of discipline or teaching techniques unless they have been trained to meet such problems or can be given special support to help cope with them.

ASSISTANCE FOR PROBATIONERS FROM THE SCHOOL AND LEA (IN THE CASE OF LEA MAINTAINED SCHOOLS)

12. The Secretary of State believes it is important for schools and LEAs to make effective arrangements for the induction of newly appointed teachers in schools. In particular –

a. Before taking up appointment the following should be made available to the probationer:

(i) the opportunity to visit the school to meet the head teacher, the head of department where appropriate and fellow members of staff;

(ii) information from the school in the form of a staff handbook or similar document giving useful facts about organisation, staff etc;

(iii) adequate notice of the timetable to be taught;

(iv) all curricular documents, including statutory documents relating to the National Curriculum, relevant to the subjects he or she will teach;

(v) information about equipment and other resources available for use;

(vi) information about support and supervision provided by the school and, in the case of LEA maintained schools, the LEA.

b. After taking up appointment the probationer should be able, so far as is practicable:

(i) to seek help and guidance from a nominated member of staff and the head of department, as appropriate;

(ii) to observe experienced colleagues teaching;

(iii) to visit other schools;

(iv) to have some of his or her teaching observed by colleagues and, in the case of teachers in LEA maintained schools, LEA advisers; to receive prompt feedback on the teaching observed; and to receive advice as necessary;

(v) to have discussions with other probationers; and

(vi) in the case of teachers in LEA maintained schools, to attend any meetings of probationers organised by the LEA.

In the case of teachers in LEA maintained schools it is important that arrangements made by LEAs and schools respectively for the training and support of new teachers should be coordinated, to avoid duplication and to provide maximum benefit for the teachers.

REPORTS ON PROGRESS

13. a. The arrangements for assessing probationers in LEAs, grant-maintained schools and non maintained special schools should be comparable and equitable as between all probationers in the LEA or school, as applicable.

b. Probationers should be made aware of the criteria on which they will be assessed. These should include class management, subject expertise, teaching skills, lesson preparation, use of resources, understanding the needs of pupils, and the ability to relate to pupils and colleagues. The statements of competence set out in Circular 18/89 on the Teachers Regulations 1989 and in the criteria for the approval of initial teacher training courses set out in Annex A to Circular 24/89 may be useful in assessing probationers' performance.

c. Each probationer should be made aware at the beginning of the probationary period of the methods of assessment to be used and the people responsible for that assessment eg. the head of department, the head teacher, and, in the case of LEA maintained schools, local authority advisers/inspectors.

d. Probationers should be told the nature of any formal assessments and have the opportunity to discuss their progress with those responsible for the assessment in time for them to heed advice before a final assessment is made.

e. Probationers should be informed at an early stage when any problems emerge which might lead to an adverse assessment. Where problems are serious they should be informed in writing. They should be warned of the consequences and be given an opportunity to heed advice . . .

EMPLOYMENT PROTECTION LEGISLATION

16. In considering any appeal against dismissal following failure of probation, Industrial Tribunals have no power to question the professional judgement of a probationer's competence, properly and reasonably exercised. However, they do take great pains to find out whether a probationary teacher has been fairly treated during probation, particularly in relation to the support given, the conditions under which the probation has been served (eg the suitability of the post(s) undertaken), and whether the probationer has had adequate advice on, and warning about, his or her performance. As part of this scrutiny Tribunals will look carefully at LEA, or, in the case of grant-maintained schools and non maintained special schools, school, policies and plans for induction and probation assessment.

This guidance from the DES was the latest in a series of administrative memoranda (the previous one had been AM no. 1/83) which had tried to regulate the relationship between the employer, the school and the new teacher and had, conspicuously, also tried to ensure a fair deal for the new teacher. In announcing his proposal to abolish the probationary period, the Secretary of State put his faith in improved arrangements for the induction of the new teacher and in 'consistent, regular cycles of appraisal' (which had become a statutory requirement for all other teachers from September 1991).

Paragraphs 6 and 7 of the letter of 17 September 1991 state (DES,1991c):

> 6. Schools with the help of their LEAs should keep a specially close eye on the work of their teachers in the first year or two of service, should assess how they are doing, should recognise achievement and help those who are struggling, and should be ready to dismiss the few who appear unlikely to become good teachers. LEA-maintained schools with delegated budgets, grant-maintained schools and non-maintained special schools can secure the removal of any teacher who falls into the latter category. Under normal employment law, any employee can be dismissed within two years of appointment without claim of unfair dismissal. The delegation of powers to individual schools also gives governors a much greater incentive to take action where performance is plainly unsatisfactory.

> 7. Against this analysis, the Secretary of State has come to the view that it is unnecessary to have a statutory arrangement for teacher probation. The essential elements for the induction and probation of new teachers are already in place and, as in other professions, need not be a legal requirement on LEAs and schools. If the Secretary of State proceeds with revocation as proposed, he will wish to consider whether to issue non-statutory guidance about probation to replace Administrative Memorandum 1/90. Consultees may wish to express views about non-statutory guidance.

Paragraph 10 explains how appraisal will be introduced for 'probationers':

> 10. The Education (School Teacher Appraisal) Regulations 1991, as currently drafted, exclude probationers from the requirement that all teachers in the maintained sector should be appraised. With the abolition of statutory probation, the Secretary of State wishes appraisal to be extended to those who would otherwise have been probationers. Appraisal can provide the springboard for the more effective induction of new teachers, allowing new teachers' development needs to be identified in a more systematic way by schools than is generally the case at present.

As noted already, this approach is fundamentally different from the intentions of Administrative Memorandum 1/90 (DES, 1990). From September 1992, then, new teachers will be drawn into the same processes of appraisal and the same constraints regarding continued employment or dismissal as all other teachers.

The change leads to even more significance being attached to the process of induction offered the new teacher. We do not yet know whether any new regulations will be introduced concerning induction. The Secretary of State suggests that he will be making recommendations about good practice (see below, and DFE, 1992b). The General Teaching Council has also published a guidance document that summarizes both academic writing and research on the subject and what is known about good practice (GTC, 1992a).

We know already that the experiences of 'starting teachers' is very different from school to school. The HMI report of 1988 contains a summary in its Table 21 (DES, 1988b: 53). While nearly all teachers reported having received support from the head, only about half the schools claimed to provide a structured induction programme (DES, 1988b: 54):

5.23 Over half of all schools claimed to provide structured induction programmes for their probationers. Among the opportunities which a majority of schools said they provided, whether the induction programmes were structured or not, were: a reduced teaching load, specifically organised meetings or discussions, the observation of the probationer's lessons, opportunities to observe lessons taught by experienced colleagues, to teach alongside other members of staff and to visit other schools.

Table 21 Arrangements after appointment: support through school programmes

Probationers:	Primary & middle %	Secondary %
take part in a structured induction programme in school	37	66
observe lessons given by experienced colleagues	66	72
teach alongside other members of staff	72	45
are observed by members of staff while teaching	89	99
have opportunities to visit other schools	71	51
attend meetings/discussions organised by school	41	80
have a reduced teaching load	39	63
experience other support arrangements	32	23

A shortage of staff and inadequate non-contact time, for example where the head had full-time charge of a class, were mentioned as reasons why the level of support was less than satisfactory.

In some secondary schools the new teachers themselves were said to produce the agendas for induction meetings and identify needs through discussion.

The LEAs, which carried responsibility for deciding on probation, also offered help. In 75 per cent of all schools, probationers were said to take part in structured induction programmes arranged by the local education authorities. The next table in the report (DES, 1988b: 55), Table 22, reports the probationers' views.

5.28 In three-quarters of all schools probationers were said to take part in structured induction programmes arranged by the local education authorities. Where probationers attended meetings arranged by the LEA, 10 per cent of primary and middle schools said the authorities arranged one meeting, usually of a general nature and offering opportunities for the new teachers to meet officers and advisers, but three-fifths described more comprehensive arrangements. Eight per cent of secondary schools referred to a single meeting and 16 per cent to at least two meetings. Three schools mentioned residential courses. Compared with 1981 many more schools reported that structured induction programmes were provided by LEAs.

Table 22 Arrangements after appointment: support from the LEA

Probationers:	Primary & middle %	Secondary %
take part in a structured induction programme provided by the LEA	77	73
attend meetings/ discussions organised by the LEA	94	89
are visited by LEA inspectors/ advisers	92	97
are observed by inspectors/ advisers in the classroom	89	94

Let us now turn to the expectations which the schools have of new teachers and what the schools think are the needs of new teachers.

WHAT THE SCHOOLS THINK ABOUT NEW TEACHERS

Schools have high expectations of new teachers. They expect 'a wide range of professional skills and personal qualities besides an awareness of current areas of development and debate' (DES, 1988b: 50). In primary and middle schools, HMI reported, emphasis was placed on professional skills such as 'classroom organisation and management, the planning and preparation of work, teaching in relation to the school's philosophy and guidelines, the ability to match tasks to the different needs of children, assessment and record keeping' (DES, 1988b: 50). There was also an expectation of strong personal qualities: 'enthusiasm, commitment and motivation, confidence, stamina, industry, co-operation, tact, good appearance, punctuality; an open, flexible, adaptable approach; and a readiness to seek, take and act on advice, learn by experience, be self-critical and express opinions' (DES, 1988b: 50).

As though this catalogue were not daunting enough, it is also clear that schools look to the newly trained teacher to bring in new ideas and perceptions, to widen the horizons of the school. And all this before the arrival of the National Curriculum. High on any list of expectations now would be capability in the subjects of the National Curriculum, with mastery or expertise in two or more.

As those who will read this in the 1990s seek their first posts, it seems clear that at least two new formal processes will be acting upon them. In the first place, the success or failure of the initial teacher training course will be judged partly or wholly by 'outcome criteria'. These will attempt to judge what the teacher 'knows', 'understands' and 'can do', presumably in both practical classroom skills and the grounding of those skills in knowledge of subject matter and children's ways of learning. In the second place, following the report commissioned by the Secretary of State in 1991, *Curriculum Organisation and Classroom Practice in Primary Schools* (DES, 1992c), and subsequent decisions by the Secretary of State and the National Curriculum Council, there will be a greater emphasis on the subject expertise of teachers in primary and middle schools and some switch in the organization of schools to allow more 'subject teaching'. The forces of control bearing on the new primary-school teacher will therefore have increased in number and changed in philosophy.

Secondary schools will probably not change so much,

although the impact of testing at Key Stage 3 and the reconceptualization of the GCSE have still to be experienced. Sound academic knowledge in their specialist subject(s) is always expected of probationers. HMI reported in 1988 that secondary schools also expected professional skills such as (DES, 1988b: 50):

> competence in basic classroom management, the ability to organise and control pupils and teach across the age and ability ranges, good planning and preparation, a range of up-to-date teaching techniques and an ability to vary teaching styles and make effective use of resources; skills in assessment, marking and record keeping; good communication and a willingness to work within departmental guidelines.

Also expected was knowledge of current areas of development, such as profiling, information technology, computer-assisted learning, school–industry links, prevocational training and modular approaches. And HMI note that the range of personal qualities expected was 'remarkably wide' (DES, 1988b: 51):

> Some of those mentioned were enthusiasm, commitment, determination, energy, confidence, open-mindedness, flexibility, humility, a sense of humour, maturity and a willingness to work hard. Probationers were expected to be self-critical, ready to discuss their difficulties openly, to take and act on advice and be willing to learn. Schools expected them to have an understanding of and sympathy with their pupils, without being too familiar, and to be able to work co-operatively in a team and to fit into the staffroom. Good standards of appearance and punctuality were also expected. A dozen secondary heads and deputy heads expected probationers to function as fully fledged teachers.

With the expectations of schools set at such a high level, the support systems offered, and described earlier, assume even greater significance. What did probationers think of them? What did schools think of their probationers? And what did HMIs think about it all?

The probationers' views of the arrangements for their induction are summarized by HMI in their Figure II (DES, 1988b: 56). In secondary schools, probationers thought they got a better deal when there was more than one of them to be considered and, presumably, the school as a whole took some responsibility rather than only a single teacher or department. In primary and middle schools, almost a fifth of new teachers were less than satisfied or dissatisfied with the support provided.

The schools were generally pleased with the skills and knowledge the new teachers brought to them. They thought 82 per cent were equipped for the job expected of them,

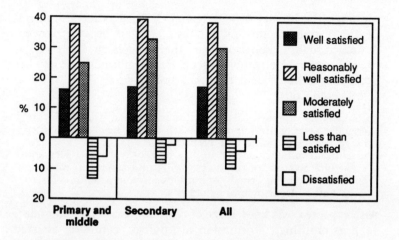

Figure II **Probationers' satisfaction with induction arrangements made by the school and the LEA.**
Source: DES (1988b: 56). Reproduced by permission of the Controller of Her Majesty's Stationery Office.

and between 92 per cent and 95 per cent of all schools were well or reasonably well satisfied with the new teachers' personal qualities and attitudes towards children, staff and the school.

HMI tried to assess whether the expectations of the schools and the assignments given probationers were reasonable, or too high or too low. These judgements probably constitute the best evidence we have for our present purpose – namely to try to help new teachers understand the extent and nature of the forces bearing upon them. The report's Tables 23–25 and 27–29 summarize HMI's judgements (DES, 1988b: 62–5). The picture is, overall, encouraging. Over 90 per cent of the appointments in secondary schools and over 80 per cent of those in primary/middle schools were 'entirely or largely appropriate'. Teachers were well equipped for their tasks and, for the most part, got adequate support from their schools. None the less, this generally rosy picture masks the facts that about

5.53 Fifty-three per cent of all schools had appropriate expectations of their new teachers. Forty per cent had expectations which were too high or rather high, and about 7 per cent had expectations that were too low or rather low.

Table 23   Schools' expectations of probationers

Schools' expectations of newly trained teachers – HMIs' assessment							Percentage of teachers
Schools' expectations were:		Rating					
		1	2	3	4	5	
too high	P	7	31	53	7	2	too low
	S	5	36	53	6	1	

5.55 Approaching half of all schools were providing either fully or substantially for the teachers' needs. About three-tenths of primary and middle schools and a quarter of secondary were providing less than adequately or not at all, suggesting that many did not appreciate the limitations of what initial training can accomplish and what induction should entail.

Table 24 Schools' provision for the needs of probationers

Schools' provision for needs of newly trained teachers – HMIs' assessment							Percentage of teachers
School has provided for needs:		Rating					
		1	2	3	4	5	
fully	P	9	37	22	27	4	not at all
	S	10	36	28	25	1	

5.58 Where primary teachers made analytical and self-critical comments in record books, these provided a basis for discussion and for heads to offer constructive advice. In secondary schools probationers in general enjoyed strong support from heads of department, particularly when these provided written as well as oral comment on lessons. Sometimes, however, there was a reluctance on the part of secondary staff to intervene where probationers clearly needed help.

Table 25 Support and advice for probationers

Support and advice for probationers – HMIs' assessments							Percentage of teachers
The probationer receives:		Rating					
		1	2	3	4	5	
(i) good support from head	P	23	29	23	21	3	no effective support
	S	11	33	24	21	9	
(ii) good support from other members of staff	P	22	38	23	13	2	no effective support
	S	31	38	16	14	1	
(iii) good support from LEA	P	5	23	30	26	16	no effective support
	S	8	12	25	36	18	

Table 25 *Cont*

Support and advice for probationers – HMIs' assessments							Percentage of teachers
The probationer receives:				Rating			
		1	2	3	4	5	
(iv) sufficient advice	P	14	33	17	23	11	insufficient
on preparation of	S	21	21	23	24	11	advice
lessons and/or schemes of work							
(v) sufficient advice	P	8	22	27	25	17	insufficient
on lesson evaluation	S	7	24	20	34	14	advice
(vi) sufficient advice	P	17	32	22	19	8	no effective
on class organisation	S	16	33	23	19	7	support
(vii) sufficient advice	P	13	36	31	15	4	insufficient
on pastoral care	S	15	32	31	16	6	advice

Table 27 The probationers' jobs: demands and opportunities

Probationers' jobs: demands and opportunities – HMIs' assessments							Percentage of teachers
The school has given this teacher a job:				Rating			
		1	2	3	4	5	
(i) more demanding	P	5	17	74	3	0	less demanding
than appropriate	S	10	37	49	3	1	than appropriate
(ii) which draws	P	13	34	38	12	3	which ignores
extensively on specific	S	32	39	21	7	1	specific skills
skills and knowledge							and knowledge
(iii) where conditions	P	16	28	21	25	10	where
encourage full	S	16	34	22	24	3	conditions fail
professional development							to provide for full professional development

Table 28 Extent to which probationers were equipped for their jobs

How well the probationer is equipped for job – HMIs' assessment							Percentage of teachers
The probationer is:		Rating					
		1	2	3	4	5	
well equipped for the job he/she has been asked to do	P	22	26	33	17	2	poorly equipped for the job
	S	19	46	21	11	1	

Table 29 Appropriateness of appointments

Appropriateness of the appointment in terms of training – HMIs' assessments							Percentage of teachers
The appointment is:		Rating					
		1	2	3	4	5	
(a) entirely appropriate to age range	P	42	26	14	9	8	inappropriate
	S	61	22	14	3	0	
(b) entirely appropriate to ability range	P	33	27	23	15	1	inappropriate
	S	45	28	17	9	1	
(c) entirely appropriate to subjects taught	P	35	29	18	15	1	inappropriate
	S	51	29	14	6	0	
(d) entirely appropriate to mix of pupils taught	P	33	32	20	14	0	inappropriate
	S	41	29	23	7	1	

a fifth of the teachers were working in conditions that failed to provide for full professional development, and that whereas three-quarters of the primary schools had given new teachers suitably demanding jobs only half the secondary schools had done so.

WORKING IN SCHOOL: INDUCTION

Thus far, we have looked at the process of getting your first teaching post, the conditions of service (employment) which will apply and the principles by which you will be appraised in your work.

You will remember that the probationary year was abolished in 1992. That makes the way in which the 'induction period' is arranged even more important. We have looked at the advice that has been given by DES to LEAs and schools about how the new probationary teachers should be helped to settle in, and we have also reviewed the findings of HMI in their two surveys of 1981 and 1987.

In making the formal announcement to do away with the probationary year, the Secretary of State also emphasized the importance of induction (DES, 1992a):

> Newly qualified teachers need properly organised introductory training and support from good experienced teachers in their first year in the classroom. This so-called induction . . . is the vital bridge between initial teacher training and professional practice . . . Induction should be a planned extension of initial teacher training . . . We must improve induction.

The Secretary of State went on to say that forty-three LEAs were being helped through Grants for Educational Support and Training (GEST) to run pilot schemes of induction and that the DES would issue new guidance. He also referred to an HMI report on LEA induction arrangements. In August 1992, the by then renamed Department for Education issued Administrative Memorandum 2/92, 'Induction of newly qualified teachers' (DFE, 1992b). It confirmed the end of probation and that the Education (School Teacher Appraisal) Regulations 1991 will apply to new teachers. Annex A offered guidance on induction, and is reproduced at the end of this chapter. Although the title has been changed from 'Assistance to the probationer' to 'Guidance to the school', it remains virtually unchanged from the 1990 version. Presumably any advice resulting from the GEST projects still lies in the future. However, sections on 'Reports on progress' and 'Employment protection legislation' (reproduced earlier in this chapter) have disappeared, indicating the new climate of teacher appraisal.

It is clear, therefore, that teachers entering service in the 1990s will experience new attempts to improve their induction and that schools will be doing this at the same time as they are introducing teacher appraisal and, in some cases, getting more involved in initial teacher training. And all this as schools continue incrementally to introduce the National Curriculum and assessment procedures, amid a restless debate about teaching and learning methods and mounting anxiety about the adequacy of school funding.

It is therefore worth taking a little time to review what we know about good arrangements for induction. A good guide is the paper prepared for the General Teaching Council Initiative by John Lambert in 1992 (GTC, 1992a). The paper (p. 23) defines induction as:

> a process which enables all new entrants to the profession to build their competence and confidence quickly. Professional self-esteem and effectiveness are its targets . . . It aims to assimilate new entrants to a particular school, to the contemporary educational scene and to a professional culture.

It should be noted immediately that this definition suggests a wider purpose than the explicitly school-centred objectives proposed in the DES press notice (DES, 1992a) and DFE Administrative Memorandum 2/92 (DFE, 1992b). There is here the notion also of induction into a professional culture set in an understanding of broad policy. In offering this definition, Lambert is drawing upon a long-established tradition of teacher training and a view of the teacher as professional rather than operator. That tension will recur at many points in this book, because it is so near the heart of our central theme: control of the service, and hence control of the teacher.

The papers published by the GTC (1992a) and the HMI report (DES, 1992b) demonstrate how much is understood about the needs of the new teacher and how sensitively and successfully these needs have been met in many LEAs and schools. The project for the next few years must be to generalize these approaches and experiences. Lambert states unequivocally that (GTC, 1992a: 27):

> Of all the factors that determine the success of induction, in the eyes of the inductees, the quality and commitment of the people who supervise them is by far the most important. It must also be said that although there is unstinted praise for good professional tutors and mentors, the most serious problems arise over inadequacies in the curriculum line manager. If relationships with that person are unsatisfactory, it is an uphill struggle for anyone else in the school.

While the school is properly the centre of care for induction, it should not try to do it all. A linking with other schools and with higher education brings essential contacts and wider horizons. This broader context, involving LEA and teacher-training institutions, can also help create a framework for assessment of the work of the new teacher, which is freed in important respects from the particularities of a single school and could provide for second thoughts and appeals. In Scotland, where teachers are registered with the General Teaching

Council, not the Scottish Education Department, the Council takes full responsibility for training in the system of assessment. The Scottish GTC makes a large commitment to induction with schools, regional authorities (LEAs) and higher education playing their parts also.

New teachers in England and Wales will need to be vigilant about the criteria by which their competences and attitudes are to be assessed, since they will almost certainly form part of a school-directed appraisal system. And, should they feel that there is something unfair or inadequate in the way the school is treating them, they should not be afraid to appeal to the wider skein of professional colleagues in LEAs and higher education.

APPENDIX

There follows an extract from the DFE's Administrative Memorandum 2/92 (DFE, 1992b), Annex A, 'Guidance on induction of newly qualified teachers (NQTs)':

Introduction

1. Local Education Authorities and Governors of maintained schools, grant-maintained schools and non-maintained special schools may wish to give all NQTs, and all those involved in the operation of induction in their schools, a copy of this guidance.

2. It would be helpful if all those having responsibility for the induction of NQTs were made aware of the findings of the HMI Report "The Induction and Probation of New Teachers 1988–1991" (Reference 62/92/NS) which was published in March 1992.

Suitable Appointments for NQTs

3. NQTs should be given an opportunity to demonstrate their proficiency in teaching classes of a size normal for the school in which they teach and the subject(s) they are teaching.

4. NQTs should be appointed to posts which are closely related to the age group and subjects for which they have been trained. This information is specified on the letters granting qualified teacher status (QTS) to those successfully completing courses of initial teacher training (ITT) or a period as a licensed teacher. Their assignments should also take account of their experience.

5. Governing Bodies and others responsible for the appointment of NQTs should try to ensure that their first teaching posts enable a reasonable assessment to be made of their conduct and efficiency as teachers and for their needs for further training to be identified and met. This is particularly important where NQTs are appointed to temporary or short-term posts.

6. The following types of post are not generally suitable for NQTs, but if they are appointed to such posts particular care should be taken to give them adequate induction and, where necessary, special support:

- posts which present unusual problems of discipline or teaching techniques;
- supply teacher posts (particular care should be taken to ensure that a regular timetable is allotted to NQTs appointed to such posts);
- peripatetic appointments, because they do not provide a stable setting in which the NQT can develop or consolidate his or her skills.

Assistance for NQTs

7. Special provision may need to be made for overseas trained teachers and those acquiring QTS through the provisions of EC Directive 89/48/EEC: induction programmes designed for NQTs trained through ITT courses in British institutions are unlikely to be suitable for such teachers.

8. Before taking up appointment the following should be made available to the NQT:

i.   the opportunity to visit the school to meet the head teacher, the head of department where appropriate and fellow members of staff;
ii. information from the school in the form of a staff handbook or similar document giving useful facts about the school's curriculum, organisation and management, staff structure, staff training and development policy, discipline, extra-curricular activities, relationships with the local community, and other relevant information;
iii. adequate notice of the timetable to be taught;
iv. all curricular documents, including statutory documents relating to the National Curriculum, relevant to the subjects he or she will teach;
v.   information about equipment and other resources available for use, including information technology;
vi. information about support and supervision provided by the school and, in the case of LEA maintained schools, any additional support provided by the LEA.

9. After taking up appointment the NQT should be able, so far as is practicable:

i.   to seek help and guidance from a nominated member of staff who has been adequately prepared for the role, and from the head of department where appropriate;
ii. to observe experienced colleagues teaching;
iii. to visit and observe teaching in other schools;
iv. to become aware of the role of their school in the local community;
v.   to have some of their teaching observed by experienced colleagues and/or LEA advisers; to receive prompt written as

well as oral feedback on the teaching observed; and to receive advice as necessary;

vi. to have regular discussions and opportunities to share experiences with other NQTs; and

vii. in the case of teachers in LEA maintained schools, to attend any meetings of NQTs organised by the LEA.

10. In the case of teachers in LEA maintained schools arrangements made by LEAs for the training and support of NQTs should supplement not duplicate provision by schools, to provide maximum benefit for the NQTs.

11. LEAs should have monitoring and reporting procedures which seek to ensure that all NQTs in schools maintained by them are known and adequately supported.

CHAPTER 3

Contracts and conditions of service

Before 1987, a teacher's contract of service was entirely deter-mined by the LEA for county, controlled and special agreement schools, and in voluntary-aided schools by the governors, though such contracts were almost invariably broadly the same as the LEA's. Salary was determined by national negotiation in the Burnham Committee, where the LEAs and teachers sat with representatives of the DES. The Secretary of State could indicate the total sum roughly available but not its detailed use in any settlement. If the Secretary of State were dissatisfied with a settlement proposed by the Burnham Committee, he could get it overturned only by a positive resolution of both Houses of Parliament – a safeguard that the LEAs and teachers had successfully had built into the 1965 Act (which had brought the DES into the Burnham negotiations for the first time since 1919). Burnham settlements always left a good deal of detail to be determined locally, so that LEAs and teacher represen-tatives were accustomed to negotiating about such aspects as special allowances, leave of absence, maternity/paternity pay and leave, etc.

From 1984 until 1987, there ensued a prolonged and bitter dispute between the DES, teachers' unions and LEAs over pay settlements and the possibility of introducing national conditions of service. In 1987, the government abolished the Burnham Committee and set up new arrangements for the determination of teachers' pay and conditions by the Teachers' Pay and Conditions Act 1987. Under this Act, salaries and conditions of service were in future to be determined by the

Secretary of State, who, after 1 October 1987, had first to seek the views of the Interim Advisory Committee. The term 'Interim' was introduced into the title in consideration of promises made during the debates in Parliament that this form of 'direct rule' was intended for only a limited period.

The Secretary of State acted swiftly. By an order promulgated before 1 October 1987, he introduced radical changes in the structure, pay and conditions of service of teachers. In other words, he created by fiat what the local authority and teachers' associations had failed to create by agreement.

The first two paragraphs of the First Report of the Interim Advisory Committee, published in March 1988, explain the new position in clear official language (Chilver Report, 1988):

> 1. The Interim Advisory Committee was established as a result of major change in the framework in which the pay and conditions of school teachers in England and Wales are determined. The Teachers' Pay and Conditions Act 1987, which had just come into force, removed the statutory basis upon which the Burnham Committee had operated. The Secretary of State was empowered under the Act to make provision by statutory order with respect to school teachers' remuneration and other conditions. The Act specifies that after 1 October 1987 such an order can be made only after he has referred the matter in question to the Interim Advisory Committee and has considered the Committee's report to him.

> 2. This was a major alteration in the framework for determining such matters; but the changes in the structure, pay and conditions of teachers which were introduced in the Secretary of State's first order under the Act were of equal consequence. The old multi-scale structure disappeared, to be replaced by a single scale for qualified classroom teachers and spot salaries for heads and deputies. A new system of incentive allowances was introduced, to be phased in over a number of years. Formal and detailed conditions of service were established for all categories of teacher, and certain reciprocal duties of their employers were also defined for the first time. The effect was to change the relationship between the contractual parties (employer and teacher), and in turn the relationship between the contractual parties and central government.

Thus, your conditions of service in school are based on the order made by the Secretary of State in 1987. The *locus classicus* is the DES publication, *School Teachers' Pay and Conditions Document 1987* (DES, 1987a), which was issued in anticipation of an order being made by the Secretary of State under Section 3 of the Teachers' Pay and Conditions of Service Act 1987. Part X of this document is entitled 'Conditions of employment of school teachers' (note the subtle change of language from 'conditions of service'). Because it is so fundamental, it is reproduced here.

Exercise of general professional duties

33. A teacher who is not a head teacher shall carry out the professional duties of a school teacher as circumstances may require –

    (1) if he is employed as a teacher in a school, under the reasonable direction of the head teacher of that school;

    (2) if he is employed by an authority on terms under which he is not assigned to any one school, under the reasonable direction of that authority and of the head teacher of any school in which he may for the time being be required to work as a teacher.

Exercise of particular duties

34. (1) A teacher employed as a teacher (other than a head teacher) in a school shall perform, in accordance with any directions which may reasonably be given to him by the head teacher from time to time, such particular duties as may reasonably be assigned to him.

    (2) A teacher employed by an authority on terms such as those described in paragraph 33(2) above shall perform, in accordance with any direction which may reasonably be given to him from time to time by the authority or by the head teacher of any school in which he may for the time being be required to work as a teacher, such particular duties as may reasonably be assigned to him.

Professional duties

35. The following duties shall be deemed to be included in the professional duties which a school teacher may be required to perform –

Teaching   (1) (a) planning and preparing courses and lessons;

    (b) teaching, according to their educational needs, the pupils assigned to him, including the setting and marking of work to be carried out by the pupil in school and elsewhere;

51

| | (c) | assessing, recording and reporting on the development, progress and attainment of pupils; |

Other activities

(2) (a) promoting the general progress and well-being of individual pupils and of any class or group of pupils assigned to him;

(b) providing guidance and advice to pupils on educational and social matters and on their further education and future careers, including information about sources of more expert advice on specific questions; making relevant records and reports;

(c) making records of and reports on the personal and social needs of pupils;

(d) communicating and consulting with the parents of pupils;

(e) communicating and co-operating with persons or bodies outside the school;

(f) participating in meetings arranged for any of the purposes described above;

Assessments and reports

(3) providing or contributing to oral and written assessments, reports and references relating to individual pupils and groups of pupils;

Appraisal

(4) participating in any arrangements within an agreed national framework for the appraisal of his performance and that of other teachers;

Review: further training and development

(5) (a) reviewing from time to time his methods of teaching and programmes of work;

(b) participating in arrangements for his further training and professional development as a teacher;

Educational methods

(6) advising and co-operating with the head teacher and other teachers (or any one or more of them) on the preparation and development of courses of study, teaching materials, teaching programmes, methods of teaching and assessment and pastoral arrangements;

Discipline, health and safety

(7) maintaining good order and discipline among the pupils and safeguarding their health and safety both when they

are authorised to be on the school premises and when they are engaged in authorised school activities elsewhere;

Staff meetings

(8) participating in meetings at the school which relate to the curriculum for the school or the administration or organisation of the school, including pastoral arrangements;

Cover

(9) supervising and so far as practicable teaching any pupils whose teacher is not available to teach them:

provided that no teacher shall be required to provide such cover –

(a) after the teacher who is absent or otherwise not available has been so for three or more consecutive working days; or

(b) where the fact that the teacher would be absent or otherwise not available for a period exceeding three consecutive working days was known to the maintaining authority for two or more working days before the absence commenced;

unless –

(i) he is a teacher employed wholly or mainly for the purpose of providing such cover ('a supply teacher'); or

(ii) it is not reasonably practicable for the maintaining authority to provide a supply teacher to provide cover; or

(iii) he is a full-time teacher at the school but has been assigned by the head teacher in the time-table to teach or carry out other specified duties (except cover) for less than 75 per cent of those hours in the week during which pupils are taught at the school;

Public examinations

(10) participating in arrangements for preparing pupils for public examinations and in assessing pupils for the purposes of such examinations; recording and reporting such assessments; and participating in arrangements for pupils' presentation for and supervision during such examinations;

53

Management	(11) (a) contributing to the selection for appointment and professional development of other teachers and non-teaching staff, including the induction and assessment of new and probationary teachers;
	(b) co-ordinating or managing the work of other teachers;
	(c) taking such part as may be required of him in the review, development and management of activities relating to the curriculum, organisation and pastoral functions of the school;
Administration	(12) (a) participating in administrative and organisational tasks related to such duties as are described above, including the management or supervision of persons providing support for the teachers in the school and the ordering and allocation of equipment and materials;
	(b) attending assemblies, registering the attendance of pupils and supervising pupils, whether these duties are to be performed before, during or after school sessions.

Working time

36.　(1) After 1st August 1987 –

(a) a teacher employed full-time, other than in the circumstances described in sub-paragraph (c), shall be available for work for 195 days in any year, of which 190 days shall be days on which he may be required to teach pupils in addition to carrying out other duties; and those 195 days shall be specified by his employer or, if the employer so directs, by the head teacher;

(b) such a teacher shall be available to perform such duties at such times and such places as may be specified by the head teacher (or, where the teacher is not assigned to any one school, by his employer or the head teacher of any school in which he may for the time being be required to work as a teacher) for 1265 hours in any year, those hours to be allocated reasonably throughout those days in the year on which he is required to be available for work;

(c) sub-paragraphs (a) and (b) do not apply to such a teacher employed wholly or mainly to teach or perform other duties in relation to pupils in a residential establishment;

(d) time spent in travelling to or from the place of work shall not count against the 1265 hours referred to in sub-paragraph (b);

(e) unless employed under a separate contract as a midday supervisor, such a teacher shall not be required to undertake midday supervision, and shall be allowed a break of reasonable length either between school sessions or between the hours of 12 noon and 2.00 pm;

(f) such a teacher shall in addition to the requirements set out in sub-paragraphs (a) and (b) above, work such additional hours as may be needed to enable him to discharge effectively his professional duties, including, in particular the marking of pupils' work, the writing of reports on pupils and the preparation of lessons, teaching material and teaching programmes. The amount of time required for this purpose beyond the 1265 hours referred to in sub-paragraph (b) and the times outside the 1265 specified hours at which duties shall be performed shall not be defined by the employer but shall depend upon the work needed to discharge the teacher's duties;

(2) in this paragraph, 'year' means a period of 12 months commencing on 1st September unless the school's academic year begins in August in which case it means a period of 12 months commencing on 1st August.

This statement remains unchanged in all essentials. It was reproduced in the Report of the Interim Advisory Committee of

31 March 1988 (Chilver Report 1988), and in DES Circular no. 10/91, 26 June 1991, 'School teachers' pay and conditions of employment' (DES, 1991a). Recommendations with regard to conditions of service are also to be found in the reports of the Interim Advisory Committee of 10 February 1989 (Chilver Report, 1989: 41-4), of 30 January 1990 (Chilver Report, 1990: 45-7) and of 18 January 1991 (Chilver Report, 1991: 43-6). At the time of writing, the latest DES publication is *School Teachers' Pay and Conditions Document 1992* (DES, 1992e).

What was essentially new in these national conditions of service, and how do they bear on our theme of 'control' – control of the service and of the teacher?

As to the system, they constituted a transfer of power from a national joint negotiating body to the Secretary of State. The general theme of the redistribution of power towards the centre will be argued more fully in Chapters 9 and 10. The government set up in 1991 a pay Review Body for teachers, intended to be independent in important respects from the Secretary of State. The impact of this new body, whose remit requires it to report on statutory conditions of employment of school teachers as well as their pay, will become apparent from 1992 onwards. In its first report, February 1992, after consideration of proposals for changes in conditions of service, the School Teachers' Review Body decided to 'recommend no changes in conditions of service this year' (DES, 1992e: para. 128).

However, it seems certain that in the future the pay Review Body will make significant proposals to vary national conditions of employment. This is so for several reasons. First, the 1991 School Teachers' Pay and Conditions Act (which provided that the Prime Minister shall appoint a review body) charged the review body with the duty of making recommendations not only on pay, 'but on those conditions of service relating to school teachers' professional duties and working time' (DES, 1992e: para. 2). Second, the Review Body's first report went on to say (para. 120):

We understand that teachers' contracts of employment will be barred, in future, from including any provisions on pay, duties and working time in addition to those specified in a Pay and Conditions Order made under the 1991 Act . . . This change in contractual arrangements reflects the changes which have taken place in the management of schools since the Education Reform Act 1988. Under local management of schools, decisions on staffing and the use of a school's resources are taken by governing bodies, but the LEA remains the employer of teachers. Were it not for the provisions of the 1991 Act, it would be open for an LEA to include in teachers' contracts such features as a limit on the size of classes to be taught, which would cut across a governing body's responsibility to manage and to take its own decisions on priorities.

That is to say, an anomaly arising from the 'double source' of employment in county schools (LEAs and governors) existing since 1988 has been resolved in favour of putting power into the hands of governors over all matters not specified in the national conditions of service. It seems certain that the actions of more than 20,000 varying governing bodies will lead to the need from time to time to lay down new or amended national conditions.

Third, it is obvious that there is already considerable pressure for changes in conditions of service. Chapter 8 of the first report of the Review Body (DES, 1992e) reported 'evidence' received from teachers' associations, the National Employers' Organization for School Teachers (NEO) and the DES. As noted, they decided to make no recommendation in 1992. But, significantly, they did say, 'We have considered carefully the evidence presented to us on these issues which we realise are of great concern to school teachers. We are by no means satisfied that all the statutory conditions are operating satisfactorily' (DES, 1992e: para. 127). They also said that some of the problems ought to be resolved by LEAs, governors and headteachers. However, it is clear that such matters as induction and performance-related pay (which affect conditions of service), as well as non-teaching staff, non-contact time and in-service training, all constitute areas to which the Pay Review Body will have to return.

As to the school, the new national conditions of service (1987) prescribed certain aspects of a teacher's work for the first time. Two of these are paramount. The 'professional duties' of a teacher are laid down in general terms. For all these, the teacher is under 'the reasonable direction of the head-teacher'. Secondly, working days and hours are prescribed. A full-time teacher must be available for work for 195 days in any year, 190 of which will be days spent in teaching pupils as well as in other duties. This introduces the notion of five days each year when teachers in a school meet, without the pupils attending, for the purpose of preparation, planning, assessment, review and in-service training. It represents an interesting compromise. Before 1987, the school had been 'required to meet' on 200 days each year, but ten of these were deemed 'occasional days' on which, for special reasons, the pupils might not attend. Some LEAs and/or governing bodies had treated the ten days virtually as additional holidays; others settled for a 5:5 split; others still were very economical with their approval of each special case offered by a school. There had, therefore, been differences between schools of up to ten days a year, and no general agreement that some of these days might be used for in-service training or other purposes, although many LEAs had begun to adopt such a policy towards the use of some of the 'occasional days'.

So, a teacher must be available for duty on 195 days each year. What of the hours per day? Again, prior to 1987 there had been differences. The DES regulations had recognized differences between primary and secondary schools; and LEAs had laid down local regulations (or had not), which had led to still further differences between schools. After 1987, any full-time teacher may be required to work for 1,265 hours per year – to be allocated 'reasonably' throughout the year. Furthermore, these 1,265 hours may be seen in three different aspects:

1   directed time – time spent on duties required by the headteacher, which may be within or beyond the 'teaching' day and on or off the school premises;
2   additional contractual obligation time: time spent discharging professional duties, including marking, preparation and writing reports, which may extend beyond the 1,265 hours and the school day;
3   self-directed time: time spent outside the teaching day and on or off the school premises.

Note that the school year is taken as normally starting on 1 September (1 August exceptionally), and that teachers are entitled to 'a break of reasonable length' either between school sessions or between the hours of 12 noon and 2.00 p.m.

At first it was thought that such detailed prescription might lead to periodic or regular disputes between teachers and heads. That has not occurred, presumably because heads have taken note of the general duty laid upon them in their conditions of service to consult staff and have behaved reasonably. Those readers who would like to see some of the detailed calculations it would be possible to make concerning teachers' duties are referred, for example, to the *Guide to School Management* (NAHT, 1991: 1.8–07–14).

More importantly, there is evidence from research that most teachers work much longer hours than their conditions of employment require. We shall examine some of this evidence now, but it is useful to bear in mind from the beginning that the chief finding is that teachers work beyond contract because of a 'conscientiousness factor'. That is, they choose to assert control in the interests of their pupils to their own personal disadvantage.

Professor Jim Campbell and Dr Sean Neill of the Education Department of Warwick University have carefully examined the workloads of teachers at Key Stage 1 (infant schools and departments) and of teachers in secondary schools. The work of teachers at Key Stage 1 was examined over two periods a year apart, which allowed the first impact of the National Curriculum, and especially the new requirements for assessment of pupils' learning, to be seen. In the case of secondary-school teachers, the National Curriculum had at that time, had little affect on workloads or patterns. In 1990, the workload of the teachers in the infant classes was fifty hours a week. A year later, it had increased to fifty-five hours a week, with the teachers of 7-year-olds working fifty-eight hours as a result of the time spent on assessment (nine hours a week), and reading the associated documentation. Campbell and Neill write (1991b):

> We can compare them with Standard Scale secondary teachers (since other secondary teachers spend more of their time on administration, which is proportionately less in primary schools). The secondary teachers spend about two hours less time per week on work overall, and about the same proportion in contact with children. They did more marking and assessment, but correspondingly less preparation than the infant teachers. The demands of infant teaching are therefore similar to those of secondary teaching, both in overall time and in the time that has to be spent away from children to prepare adequately for work with them.

So, the first conclusion to be drawn from this research is that teachers should not allow themselves to be influenced by the persistent popular opinion that in some way the teachers of young children have an easier task or work less hard than those who teach older children. In fact, both infant teachers and secondary teachers work long hours per week and, as they took the brunt of the introduction of the National Curriculum, Key Stage 1 teachers worked longer per week than their secondary counterparts.

Contracts and conditions of service: landmarks

1919–87   The Burnham Committee

1965   Remuneration of Teachers Act

1987   Teachers' Pay and Conditions Act, under which Secretary of State introduced national pay and conditions: *School Teachers' Pay and Conditions Document* (latest edition 1992)

1987–91   Interim Advisory Body (chair, Lord Chilver) – reported 1988, 1989, 1990, 1991

1991   School Teachers' Review Body (STRB) (chair, Sir Graham Day), following School Teachers' Pay and Conditions Act

1992   First Report of STRB

The second significant finding of the research is that teaching is pervaded by a vocation-driven professional attitude based in a strong personal sense in each teacher of accountability to colleagues for pupil progress. This arises from what Campbell and Neill call the 'conscientiousness factor'. They arrived at this by asking teachers what was the amount of time it would be reasonable for them to be expected to work on non-directed time. This was then compared with the time actually spent in that way. There proved to be a strong positive correlation between what teachers thought was reasonable and what they actually did: 'the more time they thought was reasonable for them to be expected to spend on work in their "own" time, the more time the teachers actually spent' (Campbell and Neill, 1991a: 42). This was equally true of both primary and secondary teachers.

This strongly suggests that teachers are motivated more by personal factors – their own views of what the task entails – than by positional factors such as status or salary. In trying to understand the levers of control in education, such a finding is highly significant. Four years after the introduction of national conditions of service, teaching had not become a contract-led profession. Teachers were working not only much longer than the requirements of directed time but also longer than they themselves considered reasonable. We shall see later that this finding sits well with a view that there is still much scope for the exercise of personal professional autonomy in teaching. What is unknown is how far the new requirements of the local management of schools, performance indicators, teacher appraisal and performance-related pay will be able to change such a culture. To the extent that they do, a significant element of control will have moved away from the individual professional towards those managing the schools and the system.

CHAPTER 4

The curriculum: the background until 1980

You may have thought, when you were yourself at school, that the curriculum was uncontroversial; it was just what you had to learn. By now, you will have realized that the question 'What should children be taught?' has become very controversial, and therefore a matter to be decided politically.

The question 'What shall be taught?' is directly related to 'Who shall be taught?', and the answer to that relates to a view of the purpose of education in society. Is it for individuals or for society, or both? Is it about fulfilment or efficiency, and *can* it be about both of those through the same means? Should it be different for some groups from others, and, if so, who is to choose the groupings?

To think about how the curriculum is controlled is therefore also to think about what those who control it think it is for. We shall now look at the various forms of control that have been exerted on the school curriculum and bring the story up to the introduction of the National Curriculum in 1988. It is important for teachers to know this history. It reveals the roots of the material they work with every day. It also gives a glimpse of the various and changing ways in which political parties have treated the meaning of 'democracy' and how democratic ideas can be fostered, shaped or restrained. This is not to suggest that anyone has thought that education was the only or even the most important influence on the next generation; but because the kind of schooling we decide to offer our young is the clearest public statement we can make about the kind of society *we* want

them to build. It is therefore a form of control across genera-
tions, and the extent to which 'liberal' or 'conservative' ideas
predominate indicates, for the time being, how much freedom
we wish to confer on those who succeed us – or indeed, what
meanings are being attached to the notion of freedom.

This is not a simple argument, as we shall see, because
some who would like to confer freedom of action see it as being
possible only if the efficiency of the economy and therefore
the capacity to create wealth is safeguarded above all; for them,
pragmatic and instrumental schooling is the way to both
efficiency and freedom. For others, such schooling is acceptable
only if it is set in a wider context of individual and social
development, and of a belief that open rather than closed ideas
represent the best hope for survival as well as fulfilment.

FROM THE REVISED CODE TO THE RUSKIN SPEECH

The school curriculum has been regulated by government and,
indirectly, by the universities for many more years than it has
been the free domain of the schools themselves. The assertion
of a national curriculum in 1988 can be seen historically as a
reversion to the norm rather than a break with 'ivy-crusted
tradition'. The Revised Code of 1863 introduced a system of
'payment by results' to the managers of elementary schools,
whose government grants thereafter depended on the performance of pupils, as assessed by HM Inspectors, according to six
standards in the 'three Rs'. Geography, language and history
were added in 1867. In that same year, Matthew Arnold in
his general report criticized the code and payment by results
(Maclure, 1968: 81–2):

> In the game of mechanical contrivances the teacher will in the end
> beat us; and as it is now found possible, by ingenious preparation,
> to get children through the Revised Code examination in reading,
> writing and ciphering, so it will with practice no doubt be found
> possible to get the three-fourths of the one-fifth of the children
> over six through the examination in grammar, geography and
> history, without their really knowing any one of these three
> matters . . . I feel sure that our present system of grants does
> harm to schools and their instruction by resting its grants too
> exclusively . . . upon individual examination, prescribed in all
> its details beforehand by the Central Office, and necessarily
> mechanical.

In fact the rigours of the Code were relaxed in 1867, and over the next thirty years the worst features of payment by results were mitigated until the principle was dropped.

Almost immediately, another form of curriculum control was introduced by government. This time, however, it was distinguished by a generosity of spirit and expressed in language of distinction. The Introduction to the *Elementary Code* of 1904 is a classic formulation of the aims of the public elementary school: it is also an enduring statement of how primary education may be envisaged (allowing for the social presumptions of a different age) and appeals still for its understanding of the importance of parents and home life (Maclure, 1968: 154–5):

> The purpose of the Public Elementary School is to form and strengthen the character and to develop the intelligence of the children entrusted to it, and to make the best use of the school years available, in assisting both girls and boys, according to their different needs, to fit themselves, practically as well as intellectually, for the work of life.

> With this purpose in view it will be the aim of the School to train the children carefully in habits of observation and clear reasoning, so that they may gain an intelligent acquaintance with some of the facts and achievements of mankind, and to bring them to some familiarity with the literature and history of their own country; to give them some power over language as an instrument of thought and expression, and, while making them conscious of the limitations of their knowledge, to develop in them such a taste for good reading and thoughtful study as will enable them to increase that knowledge in after years by their own efforts.

> The School must at the same time encourage to the utmost the children's natural activities of hand and eye by suitable forms of practical work and manual instruction; and afford them every opportunity for the healthy development of their bodies, not only by training them in appropriate physical exercises and encouraging them in organized games, but also by instructing them in the working of some of the simpler laws of health.

> It will be an important though subsidiary object of the School to discover individual children who show promise of exceptional capacity, and to develop their special gifts (so far as this can be done without sacrificing the interests of the majority of children), so that they may be qualified to pass at the proper age into Secondary Schools, and be able to derive the maximum of benefit from the education there offered them.

> And, though their opportunities are but brief, the teachers can yet do much to lay the foundations of conduct. They can endeavour, by example and influence, aided by the sense of discipline, which should pervade the School, to implant in the children habits of industry, self-control, and courageous perseverance in the face of difficulties; they can teach them to reverence what is noble, to be ready for self-sacrifice, and to strive their utmost after purity and

truth; they can foster a strong respect for duty, and that consideration and respect for others which must be the foundation of
unselfishness and the true basis of all good manners; while the
corporate life of the School, especially in the playground, should
develop that instinct for fair-play and for loyalty to one another
which is the germ of a wider sense of honour in later life.

In all these endeavours the School should enlist, as far as possible,
the interest and co-operation of the parents and the home in an
united effort to enable the children not merely to reach their full
development as individuals, but also to become upright and useful
members of the community in which they live, and worthy sons
and daughters of the country to which they belong.

The *Elementary Code* was followed up by the *Handbook of
Suggestions for the Consideration of Teachers and Others
Concerned in the Work of Public Elementary Schools*, issued
as a Blue Book by the Board of Education in 1905. The introduction turned to the teacher rather than the curriculum as
the determinant of quality and success. Again, it ranks as a
notable and enduring statement. The following extract from
the Introduction reveals the rethinking of pedagogy from
instruction towards partnership in exploration and learning,
an awareness of the crucial opportunity that only childhood
affords the human being, and the sense that 'life is a serious
as well as a pleasant thing' (Maclure, 1968: 160–1):

The Teacher and his Work. The essential condition of good education is to be found in the right attitude of the teacher to his work
. . . The teacher must know the children and must sympathize
with them, for it is of the essence of teaching that the mind of the
teacher should touch the mind of the pupil. He will seek at each
stage to adjust his mind to theirs, to draw upon their experience
as a supplement to his own, and so take them as it were into
partnership for the acquisition of knowledge. Every fact on which
he concentrates the attention of the children should be exhibited
not in isolation but in relation to the past experience of the child;
each lesson must be a renewal and an increase of that connected
store of experience which becomes knowledge. Finally all the
efforts of the teacher must be pervaded by a desire to impress upon
the scholars, especially when they reach the highest class, the
dignity of knowledge, the duty of each pupil to use his powers to
the best advantage, and the truth that life is a serious as well as
a pleasant thing.

The work of the public elementary school is the preparation of
the scholars for life; character and the power of acquiring
knowledge are valuable alike for the lower and for the higher
purposes of life, and though the teachers can influence only a short
period of the lives of the scholars, yet it is the period when human
nature is most plastic, when good influence is most fruitful, and
when teaching, if well bestowed, is most sure of permanent result.

So, for the elementary schools following the 1902 Education Act some richer ideas of what children can and should be like and what they might achieve were breaking through. It is not always remembered that the *Handbook* remained in print and continued in influence throughout the inter-war years of the 1920s and 1930s, was last revised in 1937, then after the Second World War was further revised as *Primary Education: Suggestions for the Consideration of Teachers and Others Concerned with the Work of Primary Schools*, as recently as 1959. Throughout that period it remained very influential in primary, all-age and secondary modern schools.

What of the secondary schools? The Board of Education also issued Regulations in 1904 concerning secondary schools. But their effect was not this time to encourage a broader view within a phase of education but to seek to ensure that the new county secondary schools to be established under the powers given to the newly created LEAs by the 1902 Act would follow closely the conventions and curricula of the old public and grammar schools. A different paradigm was to hand: the broader approaches, including practical and technical education, of the higher grade schools – the extended age groupings added to elementary schools by some school boards, working, it was ruled by the Cockerton judgment, outside their legal powers. But this model and its different assumptions were set aside. The history of the curriculum in England and Wales reached a turning point and failed to turn. Much of the argument over the perceived weakness of technology and science in society proceeds from that moment.

The Regulations for Secondary Schools, 1904, contained the following statement about curriculum (Maclure, 1968: 158):

> the rules . . . have been framed with the view of ensuring that the education given shall be general in its nature, while leaving greater freedom than hitherto for schools to frame curricula of varying kinds, as may be required or rendered possible by local conditions.

It goes on, however:

> A certain minimum number of hours each week must be given, in each year of the course, to the group of subjects commonly classed as 'English', and including the English Language and Literature, Geography, and History; to Languages, ancient or modern, other than the native language of the scholars; and to Mathematics and to Science.

And it ends:

Ample time is left for a well planned curriculum to add considerably to this minimum in one or more of these groups of subjects, as well as to include adequate provision for systematic Physical Exercises; for Drawing, Singing and Manual Training; for the instruction of girls in the elements of Housewifery; and for such other subjects as may profitably be included in the curriculum of any particular school.

In this way the attitudes formed in the last thirty years of the nineteenth century threw their shadow across the whole of the twentieth. Elementary schools were deemed to provide all that was needed for the great majority; hence secondary education could take on the form of a conscious minority function, oriented towards the university; and technical education was virtually ruled out of the school period and therefore destined to remain the province of low-status post-school institutions. The English have therefore periodically since been engaged in debilitating arguments about 'academic versus vocational' education, the nature of 'secondary education for all', once that became an aim after 1944, and whether 'education for capability' might not constitute a better conception of curriculum than the more usual selection of academic subjects.

The inter-war years were distinguished by a series of reports from the Consultative Committee to the Board of Education. *The Education of the Adolescent* (1926), *The Primary School* (1931) and *Infant and Nursery Schools* (1933) are known generally as the Hadow Reports, after the chairman of the Committee. They gathered together and expressed, often in the most felicitous language, the ideas about schooling which were to gather strength and largely be realized after the Second World War.

The primary-school report (Hadow Report, 1931: 91–3, all following quotations) signalled clearly that primary education must now be conceived as 'the normal way of approach to institutions for secondary education', the elementary school system, originally designed 'for the children of the labouring poor . . . in effect being reorganised out of existence'. Primary schools must 'provide a primary education in the proper sense of the term – that is, one which will be the basis for all types of higher teaching and training'. And, since so many children now attended them, 'primary schools must be considered as in principle common schools'.

Having acknowledged this dramatic structural (and social) change, the Committee turned to the curriculum. They conceived of it in terms of the development of children, consciously playing down the elementary school approach of the limited and specific. Industrialization had separated work from home, and a 'gradual apprenticeship' in the disciplines of life was no longer available to most children. 'The schools . . . have thus been compelled to broaden their aims until it might now be said that they have to teach children how to live.' The schools had accepted this with a certain 'unconscious reluctance, and a consequent slowness of adaptation'. They were good at imparting knowledge, but 'there is too little which helps children directly to strengthen and enlarge their instinctive hold on the conditions of life by enriching, illuminating and giving point to their growing experience'.

The Hadow Report went on to argue that the curriculum for pupils aged 7–11 had in many ways become distorted, and:

> so long as this is the case, it must remain important to emphasise the principle that no good can come from teaching children things that have no immediate value for them, however highly their potential or prospective value may be estimated . . . we must recognise the uselessness and the danger of seeking to inculcate what Professor A. N. Whitehead calls inert ideas – that is, ideas which at the time when they are imparted have no bearing upon a child's natural activities of body or mind and do nothing to illuminate or guide his experience.

Having analysed the situation in these terms, the Committee was ready to make a general statement about the nature of the curriculum in primary schools, one charged with significance for the post-war world and the seed-bed, still, of misunderstanding: 'Applying these considerations to the problem before us, we see that the curriculum is to be thought of in terms of activity and experience rather than of knowledge to be acquired and facts to be stored.'

Many of those who have come to see in the 'child-centred' and 'activity-based learning' approaches of the primary school a lack of intellectual and moral rigour ought to read the rest of that paragraph from Hadow. An extract makes the point. The aim of the curriculum should be to encourage the child (Hadow Report, 1931: 93):

> to attain gradually that control and orderly management of his energies, impulses and emotions, which is the essence of moral and intellectual discipline, to help him to discover the idea of duty and ensue it . . . [so as to] follow in later years the highest examples of excellence in life and conduct.

Two years later the Consultative Committee wrote about infant and nursery schools. The statement of what can reasonably be expected of a 7-year-old (Hadow Report, 1933: 145) remains valid and challenging and is expressed in wider terms than a subject-based curriculum. And the Committee concludes (Hadow Report, 1933: 145-6):

> In none of this should a uniform standard to be reached by all children be expected. The infant school has no business with uniform standards of attainment. Its business is to see that children in the infant school stage grow in body and mind at their natural rate, neither faster nor slower, . . . the only uniformity at which the infant school should aim is that every child at the end of the course should have acquired the power to attack new work and feel a zest in doing so.

The Hadow Committee had started with *The Education of the Adolescent*, begun in 1924 and published in 1926. Their consideration of the curriculum started with a complaint that sounds contemporary – and would have done to any reader this century because of the peculiarly English confusion mentioned earlier (Hadow Report, 1926: 101):

> There appear to be two opposing schools of modern educational thought, with regard to the aims to be followed in the training of older pupils. One attaches primary importance to the individual pupils and their interests; the other emphasises the claims of society as a whole, and seeks to equip the pupils for service as workmen and citizens in its organisation. When either tendency is carried too far the result is unsatisfactory . . . A well-balanced educational system must combine these two ideas in the single conception of social individuality.

So far as I am aware, the concept of 'social individuality' as the aim of schooling has never been improved upon; though admittedly it has been little understood or pursued.

As to the content of the curriculum, Hadow accepted that it would be largely subject-based, but argued for three overriding principles:

1 that the curriculum should be planned as a whole;
2 that it should be planned 'with a view to arousing interest and at the same time ensuring a proper degree of accuracy';
3 that it should be planned with local opportunities in mind and thereby 'through a liberal provision of opportunities for practical work' (Hadow Report, 1926: 104).

None the less, thinking in 1926 assumed that a minority of pupils at 11 would go forward to (Maclure, 1968: 181):

'"secondary education" in the present and narrow sense of the word' and that the rest would not. For this majority Hadow advocated 'a form of secondary education, in the truer and broader sense of the word . . . in a well-equipped and well-staffed modern school . . . under the stimulus of practical work and realistic studies, and yet, at the same time, in the free and broad air of a general and humane education, which, if it remembers handwork, does not forget music, and, if it cherishes natural science, fosters also linguistic and literary studies'.

It is difficult to escape the conclusion that those writing, who had themselves been educated in the 'narrow' tradition, found it difficult to express their meaning concisely and therefore resorted to figurative language. It is a further instance of the failure of the British education system wholeheartedly to embrace the aesthetic, technical and practical aspects of the curriculum, or the value of such studies to those whose life would be narrowed by the pursuit of 'narrow academicism'. The experience of secondary schools after 1945 made it possible to give this broader concept of secondary education much greater clarity and detail by the time the manifesto *Education for Capability* (1978; quoted in Burgess, 1986) or *Secondary Education 11–16* (DES, 1983a) were written (see also p. 76 below).

The Consultative Committee, now chaired by Will Spens, returned to secondary education in its report of 1938. Here structure preceded curriculum even more explicitly. The idea of 'multilateral schools' (that is, comprehensive schools, though with defined streams or courses) represented (Spens Report, 1938: 44):

> a policy which is very attractive; it would secure in the first place the close association, to their mutual advantage, of pupils of more varied ability . . . further, pupils could be transferred from an academic to a less academic curriculum without change of school.

However, the idea was rejected for the post-war reconstruction, and different types of curriculum for separate grammar, modern and technical high schools were envisaged instead.

Largely as a result of all the curriculum discussion of the 1920s and 1930s, when the 1944 Education Act was passed it was virtually silent about the curriculum. The experience and example of totalitarian regimes abroad had convinced a wide majority that it was a matter not to be determined centrally; after so much thinking and writing and in accordance with the ideas which prevailed, it should and could be left to the LEAs and the schools. In grammar schools, the examination system at 16 and 18 gave control enough for the purposes of employers and universities; in primary and secondary modern schools, uniformity was not a prime requirement.

The main thrust of the 1944 Act lay in new structural arrangements, not control of the curriculum. There was to be a local education authority for each area, based in local government and responsible for all education except that provided in the universities; within this, there was to be a new settlement between church schools and the state; and the minimum age at which pupils might leave school was to be raised to 15 in 1947. Most significantly for the curriculum, the parent's legal duty was changed from that of causing his or her child to receive 'efficient elementary instruction in reading, writing and arithmetic' to a duty to cause the child to receive 'efficient full-time education suitable to his age, aptitude and ability either by regular attendance at school or otherwise'. The law had almost caught up with educational thinking.

Beyond this, and the requirement for religious instruction, the curriculum was not prescribed. Section 23 of the Act put the secular instruction in county and voluntary schools under the control of the LEA. And, since Section 1 gave the Minister of Education the control and direction of the provision made by LEAs, this provided the authority needed by the government in the late 1970s when it decided to reassert its control over the curriculum. In practice after 1944, by tacit agreement, direction of the curriculum by LEAs remained a dead letter. So also did the duties laid on governing bodies of schools (see Chapter 8). On the one hand, the Ministry of Education and LEAs had other matters foremost in their minds in the period of post-war reconstruction and expansion of the school population. Building to provide 'roofs over heads', recruiting and training sufficient teachers, and then the structural reorganization of secondary education on comprehensive lines exemplify the chief concerns of central government and LEAs between the mid-1940s and the mid-1970s. On the other hand, governing bodies were relatively weak and content to leave curriculum to the teachers.

That is not to say, however, that the school curriculum was deemed unimportant or that nothing was done about it. In fact, these years of loose control saw the beginnings of the contemporary argument about the curriculum, and much national and local activity. Two separate forces were being exerted on the school curriculum, yet they interacted unavoidably. Oversimplifying, these were 'the explosion of knowledge' and the emergence of a consciously multicultural, pluralist society keen to shake off old authorities. The first created a downward pressure on the secondary schools from the universities; more and more of what had formerly been taught after school was now expected to be in the possession of pupils by the time they left school. Some agreement about criteria for selection became necessary. The still unresolved argument about the nature and content of A-level examinations is the echo of the 'big bang' of the knowledge explosion. The second force, social change, led to speculation about new kinds of valid knowledge and, especially, about new ways of teaching and learning and how to enfranchise into education groups hitherto excluded. What had seemed in the early 1950s a fairly understood, agreed and tranquil sea of curriculum had by the early 1960s become turbulent and troublesome.

The first sign of central reassertion of control came in 1962, when Sir David Eccles, the then Minister of Education, set up the Curriculum Study Group within the Ministry. Two years earlier, in the debate in the Commons on the Crowther Report about education for ages 15–19, he had said that Parliament could not dictate school curricula but it could express opinions on what was taught in schools and training colleges. In future he added, he would 'try to make the Ministry's voice heard rather more often and positively and no doubt more controversially'. It was also in this speech that he used the description of the curriculum as 'the secret garden', meaning that the schools and teachers had walled it away to themselves. Twenty years later, the Senior Chief Inspector of HMI was to remark that while HMI walked in the garden, they were not responsible for the weeds in it (and, as we shall see in a moment, by the late 1970s HMI were producing pesticidal surveys).

The reaction from teachers' associations and LEAs to the creation of the Curriculum Study Group within the Ministry was strong. They were determined to assert their stake in the process. The major outcome, following a committee of inquiry under Sir John Lockwood, was the creation in 1964 of the Schools Council for the Curriculum and Examinations. This was very different in character from the 'small but highly qualified research and development unit' which had been originally proposed by the Beloe Report in 1960. The Schools Council was to be 'a free association of equal partners, retaining unimpaired their own rights of decision within their own areas of responsibility' (quoted Nisbet, 1973). This assertion of the triangle of equal forces between central government, local government and the schools was an informing principle of the

Schools Council as it was of the education service generally after 1944. Another was the need to nurture the freedom and creativity of the individual teacher. Derek Morrell, a driving force behind both the Curriculum Study Group and the Schools Council, was a prime advocate of this, as his address to the NFER in October 1962 demonstrated (Morrell, 1963).

The history of the Schools Council from 1964 until its abolition in 1984 provides a public and conscious acting out of the problematics of the curriculum. The Council funded and organized both large-scale national projects (mathematics, English, modern languages, humanities and many others) and local initiatives. It created and sustained networks of schools, LEAs and institutes of higher education. Crucially, it linked curriculum reform with reform of the examination system. But it remained true to its origin as a child of the notion of consensus and co-operation. To the extent that the so-called 'Rank and File' movement among some teachers encouraged resistance to 'top-down' curriculum change, the Schools Council was weakened because it relied on local acceptance and action.

From another point of view, the Schools Council may also be seen as demonstrating a steady movement *away* from its founding principles towards acceptance that many others besides teachers have the right to a say in curriculum, and that it is necessary to penetrate the independence of the schools in the interests of children and society at large. Following the constitutional reforms of the mid-1970s, the Schools Council drew in representatives of parents, employers and the wider public in acknowledgement of the need for this yet wider basis for consensus. I have outlined the story elsewhere and others have written elements of it, but a comprehensive account of the significance of the Schools Council has yet to be written (Wrigley, 1970; Caston, 1971; Nisbet, 1973; Plaskow, 1985; Tomlinson, 1981). For our purpose here it is sufficient to say that it was the chief vehicle by which 'a curriculum movement' was created in Britain, a movement that was essential for the future viability of schooling, given the tensions of social change and knowledge explosion. By the 1970s these forces were already creating ideas, among both practitioners and theorists, of a common curriculum for ages 5–16.

We now come to the last chapter of the story: how a national curriculum was introduced in the 1980s.

In his speech at Ruskin College in 1976, Prime Minister Callaghan said of schooling:

73

I take it that no one claims exclusive rights in this field. Public interest is strong and legitimate and will be satisfied. Parents, teachers, learned and professional bodies, representatives of higher education and both sides of industry, together with the government all have an important part to play in formulating and expressing the purpose of education and the standards that we need.

It set the agenda for the next fifteen years. We shall now see how the DES reminded – goaded – LEAs about their responsibilities for the curriculum, made its first faltering steps towards a national framework for the curriculum (1980a), attempted, in *Better Schools* (1985e), to make a final declaration of belief in the efficacy of partnership and then, from 1987, finally and coldly set aside that belief and introduced the National Curriculum by government fiat.

A little more of the context for the period 1976–88 must be put in place before that story is told. Besides the public and political concern expressed in the Ruskin speech and subsequently in the 'Great Debate' and the Green Paper *Education in Schools* (DES, 1977b) that followed it, there was also professional concern about some aspects of the curriculum. This was put unequivocally in two HMI reports based on surveys of primary schools (1978) and secondary schools (1979). *Primary Education in England* (DES, 1978a) showed that in primary schools the 'three Rs' were attended to and well taught, reading standards continued an upward trend since the war and 'progressive' methods had not run wild – 75 per cent of teachers used mainly didactic methods, only 5 per cent mainly 'exploratory' and 20 per cent a combination of both. Most significant of all, the results in pupil learning were best where the curriculum was broad; there was no case for narrowing the curriculum in order to raise standards. And yet the general class teacher was not coping well enough in trying to teach all subjects of the curriculum. Science was badly taught and often neglected. The humanities were not strong enough. The beginnings of the advocacy of specialism among primary teachers were discernible and the idea of 'curriculum leaders', already suggested for English in the Bullock Report (DES, 1975), emerged clearly.

The report on secondary education, *Aspects of Secondary Education in England* (DES, 1979a: 265), showed that 'Thirty-five years after the 1944 Act the education system is still seeking to give effect to the commitment of that Act to secondary education for all.' Ideas of secondary education had very much enlarged, pupils stayed in it longer and there was greater understanding of how children learn. In short, the challenge and complexity had greatly increased and 'there are no once-for-all prescriptions to be sought or found' (DES, 1979a: 226):

> 'The curriculum' has no nationally defined content in this country, but at institutional level it has broadly similar connotations. This broad simplicity is not true for the pupils. For them, certainly from the fourth year and sometimes earlier, the curriculum consists of a number of building blocks, some with a fine patina of tradition, some still comparatively novel, with very few rules governing their selection and assembly . . . the resultant individual programmes may still display marked disparities in the range and quality of experience they signify.

The reasons for this break at age 14 were the way in which the school leaving age had been raised in stages from 14 to 16 and the single-subject examination system: 'An à la carte examinations system sits more comfortably on an à la carte curriculum.' And then the verdict (HMSO, 1979: 266):

> It is easy, then, to appreciate how schools come to be as they are. But the evidence of this survey is that many pupils are not well served by the curricular structures and organisation of their schools. Some are deprived . . . of important areas of experience . . . both the more able and less able pupils . . . Others . . . are not readily enabled to relate what they learn in different subjects or to see applications in new contexts.

In short, the secondary schools needed more whole-curriculum planning and much less complexity and incoherence, especially for pupils beyond age 14.

These two surveys had been instituted by the Senior Chief Inspector in 1974/5, and their findings that there was an 'unacceptable diversity' in curriculum were coming through to the Inspectorate and those working with them in DES and LEAs at the time of the Ruskin Speech and beyond. Indeed, a month before James Callaghan's speech, some HMI and five LEAs had established the major curriculum development and school review project which gave rise to the 1977–83 publications on *Curriculum 11–16* (DES, 1977c, 1979c, 1983c), and which were to prove very influential in the 1980s. Likewise, serious attempts to introduce science to the primary schools and strengthen the teaching of history and geography gathered increasing momentum from 1978.

There was not only political and professional concern about the curriculum evident by the late 1970s; it had also become discernible among leaders in industry, commerce and the public services, who joined with figures in the education world to produce a manifesto, *Education for Capability*. This captured well the way in which it was felt that too much concentration on academic and analytical aspects of learning at the expense of creative approaches to 'real' problems had distorted the education of all our people, not least those who subsequently achieved positions of power and authority. This is what the manifesto said (Burgess, 1986: frontispiece):

> There is a serious imbalance in Britain today in the full process which is described by the two words 'education' and 'training'. The idea of the 'educated person' is that of a scholarly individual who has been neither educated nor trained to exercise useful skills; who is able to understand but not to act. Young people in secondary or higher education increasingly specialize, and do so too often in ways which mean that they are taught to practise only the skills of scholarship and science. They acquire knowledge of particular subjects, but are not equipped to use knowledge in ways which are relevant to the world outside the education system.

> This imbalance is harmful to individuals, to industry and to society. A well-balanced education should, of course, embrace analysis and the acquisition of knowledge. But it must also include the exercise of creative skills, the competence to undertake and complete tasks and the ability to cope with everyday life; and also doing all these things in co-operation with others.

> There exists in its own right a culture which is concerned with doing, making and organizing and the creative arts. This culture emphasizes the day-to-day management of affairs, the formulation and solution of problems and the design, manufacture and marketing of goods and services.

> Educators should spend more time preparing people in this way for a life outside the education system. The country would benefit significantly in economic terms from what is here described as Education for Capability.

This manifesto spoke also for those in the curriculum movement who believed that there are many kinds of human intelligence, many ways of knowing and each with its own tests for truth, and that curriculum should reflect and reinforce that variety. The strength of language and concept indicates that ideas and practice had become stronger and clearer since, for example, the Hadow Committee in 1926 had had to resort to the use of figurative language in describing the curriculum for the modern secondary schools which it advocated.

THE BEGINNING OF THE END OF CURRICULAR FREEDOM IN SCHOOLS

Seen against this background of political, professional and social concern, the government's increasing assertion of control over curriculum from 1977 is intelligible. The Green Paper *Education in Schools*, of July 1977 (DES, 1977b), announced the government's intention to ask all LEAs to review and report upon their 'curricular arrangements'. Circular 14/77, issued in November 1977, instituted this with a detailed and intimidating catechism. While the results were being collected and analysed, the Callaghan government was replaced by that of Margaret Thatcher, but as in much else in education this strand of policy carried over, and in November 1979, the new Secretary of State, Mark Carlisle, issued *Local Authority Arrangements for the School Curriculum* (DES, 1979b). It reads now as the epitaph for the thirty years of curricular freedom for schools and LEAs.

At the time, the DES and everyone else tried to capture both the findings and the urgent action they clearly demanded within the current structure of DES/LEA/school partnership (DES, 1979b: 2):

> The Secretaries of State do not intend to alter the existing statutory relationship between these various partners . . . with responsibilities for school education: central and local government, school governing bodies and teachers . . . Indeed they believe that the effective development and implementation of curricular policies must be based upon a clear understanding of, and must pay proper regard to, the responsibilities and interests of each of the partners and the contribution which each can make.

However, the harbingers of greater central control are there to discern. The first and crucial question was, 'What procedures have the authority established to enable them to carry out their curricular responsibilities under Section 23 of the Education Act 1944?' The Report recorded that (DES, 1979b: 14):

> Two-thirds of authorities included in their answer to this question, or in a covering letter to their response as a whole, a statement explaining that the authority (as one typical reply put it) 'has not established and would not wish to see develop, a formal system of detailed control over the curriculum of individual schools'.

LEAs pointed to the duties and responsibilities of governing bodies and said that 'in practice most curricular matters were left to the head teacher and other members of the teaching

---

The curriculum: the background until 1980: landmarks

Government control

    1863   The Revised Code

Greater freedom for teachers

    1902   Education Act
    1904   *Regulations for Secondary Schools*
    1904   *The Elementary Code*
    1905   *Handbook for Elementary School Teachers*
              (revised and reissued 1937 and 1959)

The inter-war years: curriculum debate

    1926   Hadow Report: *The Education of the Adolescent*
    1931   Hadow Report: *The Primary School*
    1933   Hadow Report: *Infant and Nursery Schools*
    1938   Spens Report: *Secondary Education*

1944 Education Act

The years of debate and concern

    1959   Crowther Report: *Education 15–18*
    1962   Curriculum Study Group
    1964   The Schools Council for Curriculum and
              Examinations
    1969   The first Black Paper
    1976   The Ruskin Speech
    1977   *Education in Schools* – Green Paper
1977–83   HMI/LEA Curriculum 11–16 Project
    1978   Education for Capability Manifesto
    1978   HMI Report: *Primary Education in England*
    1979   HMI Report: *Aspects of Secondary Education in
              England*
    1979   *Local Authority Arrangements for the School
              Curriculum*

---

staff'; in other words, the position was as the Taylor Committee had also found (see Chapter 8). However (DES, 1979b: 14):

> many authorities considered that this general delegation did not prevent them from exercising curricular responsibilities, most commonly through a process of consultation, guidance and support, but sometimes more directly, through the issue of policy statements . . . authorities saw these activities as important parts of their duties.

Nevertheless, in sum, only one-fifth of LEAs could report that they had studied various aspects of curricular provision in this way.

The problem was exacerbated by the answers to the question, 'What curricular elements do the authority regard as essential?' As the Report put it (DES, 1979b: 49):

> The nature of the problem was encapsulated in the passage of Aristotle quoted by one authority: 'People do not agree on the subjects which the young should learn . . .; nobody knows whether the young should be trained at such studies as are merely useful as a means of livelihood, or on such as tend to the promotion of virtue, or in the higher studies . . .' In fact most responses conveyed the view that the curriculum ought to consist of a balance of these and other elements, although authorities expressed this opinion in differing ways and with differing emphasis.

Although 20 per cent of LEAs did not wish to direct the curriculum, the rest presented a rich account of curriculum ideas and practice which stands testimony to the curriculum debate, both academic and practical, that had characterized the previous twenty years. The problem, since so it now appeared to be, was diversity and variety. Circular 14/77 and the Report of 1979 provided the mirror image in administration to the two HMI surveys of 1978 and 1979 (DES, 1978a, 1979a). The stage was set for intervention by central government. Indeed, the Report on Circular 14/77 made the intention explicit (DES, 1979b: 6): 'The Secretaries of State . . . believe they should seek to give a lead in the process of reaching a national consensus on a desirable frame-work for the curriculum.'

CHAPTER 5

The curriculum: the 1980s and after

1980–8

This crucial period begins with a mouse and ends with a lion. The mouse was *A Framework for the School Curriculum* (DES, 1980a) and the lion the Education Reform Act of 1988. *A Framework for the School Curriculum* was published as a consultation paper by the DES in January 1980. It claimed to be the government's 'preliminary views on the form that framework should take and the ground it should cover'. Again, it was declared that there was no intention to change the law. But curricular responsibilities needed to be more clear, and new imperatives were added to those already declared: 'falling school rolls and the need to limit public expenditure make it more important to establish priorities' (para. 3).

For the first time, it was proposed that the LEA 'should have a clear and known policy for the curriculum offered in its schools'. The 'aims' of the school curriculum were reduced from the eight proposed in *Education in Schools* (DES, 1977b) to six. The casualties were the education of children 'whose social or environmental disadvantages cripple their capacity to learn' and the 'search for a more just social order'. Then, again for the first time in the post-1944 period, appeared an explicit list of subjects: English, mathematics, science, modern languages, physical education and religious education; beyond this, 'preparation for adult and working life'. It was an impoverished view of the curriculum and made to look even more so because, the day following (publication had been deliberately delayed), HMI produced *A View of the Curriculum* (DES, 1980b), which offered not only a deeper analysis and more generous conception but also a view grounded in the HMI surveys.

The reaction to *A Framework* was strong and antipathetic. The DES set up special procedures to produce something more substantial from the consultation process. The Schools Council had decided in 1979 that it must produce a statement about the whole curriculum for ages 5–16. The government's document, as the sequel to *A Framework*, suffered a good deal of delay and the Schools Council Chairman was asked to hold back the Council's document until the government's was ready. HMI and DES officials had been members of the Council's working party: there had been no secrecy between Council and DES and the request was granted. In the event, *The School Curriculum* (DES, 1981) and *The Practical Curriculum* (Schools Council, 1981) were both published in March 1981.

The DES document was fuller than *A Framework* of 1980, less prescriptive in tone, admitted questions which needed further consideration, acknowledged the work done and in hand, and maintained the idea of partnership. Schools and LEAs should analyse and set out clearly their curricular aims, but 'Neither the Government nor the local authorities should specify in detail what the schools should teach' (DES, 1981: 3).

Not everyone in government, however, was content with that approach. The next intervention came not from the DES but from the Department of Employment, through the Manpower Services Commission. The Technical and Vocational Education Initiative (TVEI) was announced in 1982 by David Young, Secretary of State for Employment, with the support of the Prime Minister and without prior consultation with DES officials. It owed more to the *Education for Capability* strand of curriculum thinking than to the current DES approaches. It was to apply to the age-group 14–18, whether in schools or in further education. It provided additional money specifically to achieve such objectives as work experience, the teaching of technology, and new forms of active learning. It was extended in 1985 to all students aged 14–18, before the evaluation reports on the pilot schemes of 1983–5 were available. The 1985–95 main phase was to cost £900 million. It is unquestionably the largest single curriculum development project ever funded or attempted in Britain. It was well under way when, in 1987, the DES announced plans for a national curriculum conceived in the other, subject-based, tradition.

That, combined with changed policies in the Department of Employment which led to the disappearance of the powerful Manpower Services Commission, caused TVEI to be changed from a process intended to introduce technical and vocational elements into the school curriculum into a weaker process mainly concerned with the methods of learning. This was paralleled by new explanations for British economic weakness emanating from government, 'no longer focused upon deficits in our technological education and training but rather upon lack of enterprise and the isolation of the education system from industry and commerce' (Merson, 1992). TVEI was thus marginalized in the late 1980s and the way cleared for a quite different basis of government intervention into the curriculum, through the resurgent Department of Education and Science.

During Sir Keith Joseph's time at the DES (1982-6), the attempt to find a sharper definition of the school curriculum within the notion of partnership continued. *Better Schools* (DES, 1985e) devoted a lengthy chapter to 'The primary and secondary curriculum'. It argued that consultation with 'the Government's partners' had shown, that 'broad agreement about the objectives and content of the school curriculum is a necessary step' towards raising standards (para. 30). Such explicit agreement would bring five advantages (para. 31):

1   It would clarify 'what tasks society expects our schools to accomplish'.
2   Parents, employers and public would be able to understand better what schools were doing and therefore be able to support them better.
3   The expectations teachers had of their pupils would be raised.
4   It would prevent standards in any locality falling below an acceptable level.
5   It was a prerequisite for monitoring achievement and progress.

'The Government acknowledges the magnitude of the task it is setting itself and its partners. Objectives cannot be agreed for all time. Even initial agreement will take several years to accomplish although some objectives may be settled sooner' (para. 32).

Better Schools then ventured into discussion of curriculum content. In the primary phase, nine broad objectives were proposed. They can be seen now as prefiguring the nine subjects of the National Curriculum, together with cross-curricular themes such as moral education, information technology and insight into the adult world. At the time, both the drafters and the readers were clear that they wanted to eschew a subject-described curriculum in primary schools. At the secondary stage, subjects were more salient. The underlying concept was of a common curriculum for the first three years, with choice from 14 to 16 constrained by the need for breadth and balance. *Better Schools* stated (para. 68):

> Alongside and through these elements, here expressed in terms of subject areas, the 11-16 curriculum should continue the work of the primary phase in developing positive personal qualities and attitudes, consolidating pupils' understanding of the values and foundations of British society, and fostering social and study skills. The ethos of a school and the moral education it provides also play a significant part in reinforcing attitudes and behaviour.

The dynamic of the curriculum was recognized (para. 85):

> The school curriculum is not static. It is constantly being developed as teachers individually and collectively reappraise what they teach and adapt the existing or the new tools of their trade in response to changes in the needs of their pupils, the state of knowledge, ideas and attitudes in society, and their perceptions of these matters. Curriculum development is a professional activity, consciously and deliberately carried out by teachers and others.

The next steps towards the nationally agreed curriculum framework, *Better Schools* announced, would consist of a further account of LEA practice (following DES Circular no. 8/83, which had called for further reports from LEAs (DES, 1983c)) consultations about individual subjects and further papers from HMI and others on curriculum 5-16.

Better Schools marks the high tide of the attempt to achieve a national curriculum within the partnership of central government, LEAs and schools. In the same month, DES published the HMI document *The Curriculum from 5 to 16* (DES, 1985d), which represents the best professional commentary on school curriculum yet written. It embraced primary, secondary and special education. It drew heavily upon the traditions of primary practice and the research and development of the Curriculum 11-16 Project. It conceptualized the curriculum as having two essential and complementary perspectives: first, the *areas of learning and experience*, and second, the *elements of learning*, that is, the knowledge, concepts, skills and attitudes to be developed. Conceived like this, the curriculum can make use of the way in which knowledge

83

is organized as 'subjects' but escape both the tyranny and narrowness of a curriculum based solely in subjects. Areas of experience are the domains through which humankind has gained access to understanding of itself and the world. Any particular subject will contribute to more than one of these areas in differing magnitudes. It is possible for teachers at a school to examine the content of each subject of the curriculum, for each stage, in terms of its contribution to the areas of experience (aesthetic and creative, human and social, linguistic and literary, mathematical, moral, physical, scientific, spiritual and technological). It is important, then, to 'measure' the balance of the curriculum in terms of the nine areas of experience rather than of subjects. Moreover, this insight also makes allies of subject teachers who otherwise may proclaim and defend their particularity. It is a unifying way for a school staff to look at their work and not only allows them to examine balance, at any one stage and over a course of several years, but also coherence and progression, two other essential requisites of the school curriculum.

The elements of learning proposed in *The Curriculum from 5 to 16* are knowledge, concepts, skills and attitudes. To analyse a school curriculum from these standpoints is to understand much more clearly what it is expected the pupil will learn and, crucially, to get a clearer idea about what it is assumed he or she already knows, can do or understands. In this way, we move towards a more satisfactory definition of curriculum as what the pupil receives rather than what the teacher transmits.

In his covering letter to chief education officers, the Senior Chief Inspector said about *The Curriculum from 5 to 16*, 'It does not prescribe a single framework, as other approaches might be equally valid. But whatever framework is adopted for planning and analysis, schools need to face the issues which the document raises.' In other words, like *Better Schools* but from the professional standpoint, *The Curriculum from 5 to 16* was positioned firmly in the tradition of devolved control of the curriculum, but asserting a sharper and more intellectually worked out analytical framework; in future, LEAs and schools would have to show they had applied this or offer one of their own, equally forceful, instead. It was a potential moment of equipoise in the development of control over the school curriculum. Had it continued, the quality of thought and action at all three levels – central, LEA and school – might have been stimulated into continual improvement. But political events swept it aside and the National Curriculum of 1988 supervened.

Sir Keith Joseph was succeeded as Secretary of State for Education by Kenneth Baker, and a different kind of new right radicalism was asserted. Keith Joseph believed in the wisdom of the market and was opposed to centralist prescriptions. He spoke against the National Curriculum in the debates in the Lords during the passage of the 1988 Reform Act. Kenneth Baker was a modernizer as well as a marketeer. His Reform Act therefore both extended market principles of choice and diversity and at the same time introduced a national curriculum in order to be rid of the diversity of curriculum still apparent between and within LEAs and schools. The paradox made those who welcomed the idea of a national curriculum as furthering and establishing in law, for the first time, the child's right of access to an agreed curriculum fearful that the diversity of schools and approaches required by the market would make the entitlement to curriculum merely a façade. Events since, not least John Patten's promotion of grant-maintained schools with specialist aspects and his interventionist proposals for 'turning round' 'failing schools', have fully justified those anxieties. None the less, the idea of a national curriculum was one whose time had come by the late 1980s in Britain. It represented the furtherance of the pursuit of equity; and a necessary clarification of purpose and content which would allow the central professional debate usefully to shift to methods of teaching and assessment. The argument was about the extent and detail of the prescription; it still is, and must remain so for as long as we care about what children should be required to learn and why.

INTRODUCING THE NATIONAL CURRICULUM

Probably the first public announcement that a third Thatcher administration, if elected, would introduce a 'national core curriculum' was made by Kenneth Baker in early December 1986 when he was interviewed by Matthew Parris on ITV's *Weekend World* programme. He elaborated his ideas in two speeches during January 1987. At the North of England Education Conference, he described the English education system as 'a bit of a muddle' and compared it unfavourably with those of most European countries, which had 'tended to centralise and standardise. We have gone for diffusion and variety. In particular, the functions of the State have largely been devolved to elected local bodies; and the school curriculum has largely been left to individual schools and teachers' (DES, 1987c). That is, the responsibilities of LEAs and the curricular freedom of schools would be reduced as central controls increased: the days of partnership were over. The Secretary of State took the opportunity to press the message home even more firmly later in January 1987 at the Conference of the Society of Education Officers – that is, to those serving in the LEAs. He would not be diverted by the views of 'professional educators' (DES, 1987c):

> I believe that, at least as far as England is concerned, we should now move quickly to a national curriculum . . . I believe profoundly that professional educators will do a disservice to the cause of education, and to the nation, if they entrench themselves in a defence of the *status quo*. More and more people are coming to feel that our school curriculum is not as good as it could be and needs to be, and that we need to move nearer to the kind of arrangements which other European countries operate with success.

In advance of any legislation, the Secretary of State's next step was to set up two working groups, on mathematics and science, in April 1987. They were to advise the government on attainment targets suitable for children of differing ages and abilities, and the programmes of study which would allow them to be achieved. 'Clear and challenging attainment targets were needed for the key ages of seven, eleven and fourteen' so that from them could be derived 'the essential content, skills and processes to be taught in each subject' (DES, 1987e). In this way the language of 'attainment targets' and 'programme of study' arrived in advance of the legislation of 1988, as did the salience of assessment.

The Conservative government was re-elected in June 1987. The Conservative Party's election manifesto (p. 18) had reiterated the intention to introduce a national curriculum and had promised, 'We will consult widely among those concerned in establishing the curriculum.'

The DES published *The National Curriculum 5–16: A Consultation Document*, in July 1987 (DES, 1987b). The government's objective was a 'school curriculum which will develop the potential of all pupils and equip them for the responsibilities of citizenship and for the challenges of employment in tomorrow's world' (para. 4). The document went on to present the case for a national curriculum. There was general agreement about the aims for education that had been set out in *Better Schools* (DES, 1985e), but progress had been variable, and standards needed to be raised consistently, 'and at least as quickly as they are rising in competitor countries' (para. 6). Then came the appeal to equity: 'Pupils should be entitled to the same opportunities wherever they go to school' (para. 7). Standards would be raised through a broad and balanced curriculum, the setting of clear objectives, and checking on progress. Furthermore, pupils would be able to move from one area to another with minimum disruption of their education. Schools would become more accountable and employers would have a better idea of what school leavers had studied and learnt.

The curriculum itself was defined almost entirely in terms of academic subjects. Mathematics, English and science would form the core, with technology, history, geography, art, music, physical education and (after 11) a modern foreign language as the other foundation subjects. Time would not be prescribed, 'But the foundation subjects commonly take up 80–90 per cent of the curriculum where there is good practice' (para. 16). In secondary schools, 30–40 per cent of curriculum time should be given to the three core subjects (para. 15). Besides the subjects (para. 18):

> there are a number of subjects or themes, such as health education and the use of information technology, which can be taught through other subjects . . . it is proposed that such subjects or themes should be taught through the foundation subjects, so that they can be accommodated within the curriculum but without crowding out the essential subjects.

That is, the curriculum would be almost entirely subject-defined, backed by programmes of study and attainment targets.

These proposals were recognized by both professional and lay public as radical. The curriculum consultative document attracted about half of the more than 20,000 responses received in Whitehall to the half-dozen or so papers which were published as a prelude to the 1988 Reform Act – all issued during the summer holiday season and with responses required by mid-September. The extent and weight of the responses took ministers and civil servants by surprise. As Stuart Maclure puts it, 'there must be some scepticism as to how closely they studied the tens of millions of words which descended on them while they were already heavily engaged in drafting the Bill' (Haviland, 1988: xi). In the event, the government decided not to publish any of the responses received. We know of their general tenor, however, because of *Take Care Mr. Baker*, a compilation of extracts edited by Julian Haviland and drawn from the copies deposited in the library of the House of Commons. Lawton and Chitty, who evidently did not use Haviland's work, say that 'the consultation document was greeted with a chorus of disapproval and disbelief from educationists, teachers and union leaders alike' (Lawton and Chitty, 1988). How can this be if, as I suggested earlier, a large measure of professional support had gathered around the idea of a national curriculum by the mid-1980s?

There may be explanations. First, a distinction needs to be drawn between those who had been involved in the curriculum movement at the national level and those whose work had been grounded mainly or entirely in school or college, university or LEA. The former group, for the reasons explained in this chapter, were generally minded to support a national curriculum, although there would have been much less agreement about the detail. Second, primary-school teachers generally found a curriculum described in subject terms both alien and inappropriate. The younger the age-group of children in consideration, the stronger was this view. Secondary-school teachers generally opposed a national curriculum because of the prescriptiveness and control it represented. Many active and concerned teachers of pupils aged 14 and over had been engaged in loosening the grip and avoiding the prescriptiveness of some public examination syllabuses and had developed Mode III syllabuses which took account of new kinds of knowledge, new ways of teaching and new ways of assessing achievement. Besides these anxieties, all educationists, including those who favoured a national curriculum, were at a loss to know why the approach to the curriculum represented by thinking of it as access to the areas of experience had been ignored. It had been eloquently placed in the literature in *The Curriculum from 5 to 16* (DES, 1985d) and *Curriculum 11–16* (DES, 1983a). Lastly, all working in education were disturbed by the consultative document's scant regard for social and personal development, economic and political understanding and moral education.

The Education Reform Bill was therefore put before Parliament in November 1987 against a background, so far as the curriculum was concerned, of controversy, even anger, and with many who might otherwise have supported being opposed to the government's proposal.

THE 1988 EDUCATION ACT

The debates in both Lords and Commons on the Education Reform Bill were long and bitter. However, the essential structure proposed for the National Curriculum survived almost unchanged. The most important additions were a ringing opening statement about the general purposes of education, which echoed and reinforced that of the 1944 Act, and requirements resulting from eleventh-hour amendments in the Lords concerning collective worship and religious education. We can, therefore, turn to the terms of the Act in respect of school curriculum. Emphasis is placed here upon the procedure by which the curriculum (that is, programmes of study and attainment targets) is given the force of law. This is the procedure that has to be used for every amendment also, and the period since 1988 has already seen numerous detailed changes in both the curriculum and the assessment procedures. From the viewpoint of understanding how government controls the school curriculum, it is the procedure that matters, and especially the points at which consultation is required and explanations have to be given if advice is not heeded. The prime source is, of course, the Act itself, but it is also helpful to follow the DES Circular no. 5/89 (DES, 1989e).

The aims of the school curriculum

Section 1 of the Act tries to place the curriculum within the broad context of the needs of society and of the pupils. It says that the curriculum should be balanced and broadly based, and should

(a) promote the spiritual, moral, cultural, mental and physical development of pupils at the school and of society; and
(b) prepare such pupils for the opportunities, responsibilities and experiences of adult life.

Circular no. 5/89 explains the force of this clause as follows:

17. This restates and extends the list of central purposes for the curriculum in Section 7 of the 1944 Act; in particular, it emphasises the need for breadth and balance in what pupils study, and that cultural development and the development of society should be promoted. It is intended that the curriculum should reflect the culturally diverse society to which pupils belong and of which they will become adult members. It should benefit them as they grow in maturity and help to prepare them for adult life and experience – home life and parenthood; responsibilities

as a citizen towards the community and society nationally and internationally; enterprise, employment and other work. The requirements of Section 1 apply to *all* pupils – regardless of age – registered at *all* maintained schools, including grant-maintained schools, except that they do not apply to pupils in nursery schools or nursery classes in primary schools.

The structure of the National Curriculum

The *basic curriculum* is made up of religious education and the National Curriculum. The *National Curriculum* comprises core and other foundation subjects, namely:

- *core subjects*: Mathematics, English, science;
- *other foundation subjects*: history, geography, technology, music, art and physical education for all stages; and, for pupils in Key Stages 3 and 4, a modern foreign language.

For each subject there will be (Circular no. 5/89, para. 23):

i *Attainment targets*, defined as the knowledge, skills and understanding pupils are expected to have by the end of each key stage. They will provide objectives for what is to be learned in each subject during that stage;

ii *Programmes of study*, defined as the matters, skills and processes which must be taught to pupils during each key stage. They will set out the essential ground to be covered in order to meet the objectives set out in the attainment targets; and

iii *Assessment arrangements*, defined as the arrangements for assessing pupils at or near the end of each key stage, for the purpose of ascertaining what they have achieved in relation to the attainment targets for that stage.

How are the attainment targets, programmes of study and assessment arrangements to be decided? The final point in the process is an Order made by the Secretary of State – that is, a Statutory Order, made under the authority of the Act; it has to be laid before Parliament and assumes the force of law once it has been approved (positive affirmation) or once the necessary time has elapsed for any member of either House to raise an objection (negative affirmation). It is, in effect, a purely formal procedure. So, once the Order is made, the schools (and the Secretary of State, the LEA and the governing body) have a legal duty to discharge their responsibilities in such a way that the terms of the Order are fulfilled.

Section 20 of the 1988 Act specifies the consultations which must occur in England before any Order to amend the list of foundation subjects and Key Stages, or to specify attainment targets or programmes of study. The National Curriculum Council (created by the Act) is given a central role in carrying out these consultations and in giving advice to the Secretary of State, who has to publish a statement of his or her reasons for any departure from the National Curriculum Council's advice. The procedure by which we arrive at a programme of study or attainment targets is broadly as follows:

1   A working group is set up by the Secretary of State.
2   The working group reports to the Secretary of State.
3   The Secretary of State refers the report to the National Curriculum Council, together with any comments he or she may wish to make at that point.
4   The National Curriculum Council arranges statutory consultations.
5   The National Curriculum Council reports back to the Secretary of State. It is obliged to offer:

    – a summary of the views expressed during consultation;

    – its recommendations on the proposals;

    – any other advice it may wish to offer.

6   The National Curriculum Council is obliged to publish its report to the Secretary of State (so that it becomes part of the public literature).
7   A Draft Order is then issued by the Secretary of State and on this there must be a further round of consultations. At this point, the Secretary of State must:

    – publish the Draft Order along with reasons for any failure to take National Curriculum Council advice;

    – send copies to the National Curriculum Council and all those consulted by it; and

    – allow at least one month for further evidence and representations.

8   The Order may then be made by the Secretary of State, with or without modifications.

The Parliamentary procedure which applies is laid down in Section 232, namely, an affirmative resolution for amendments to the foundation subjects or Key Stages (other than the redefinition of the boundary between first and second Key Stages in relation to individual subjects), and a negative resolution for all other orders.

Matters not included in the National Curriculum

In view of the degree of prescription contained in the National Curriculum, it may be helpful to end this chapter by looking at the areas of 'freedom' given to the schools (that is, still available as a continuation of the pre-1988 situation). First, the vexed issue of the time to be spent on various parts or subjects was left open. The Act relies on the concepts of 'reasonable time' to create 'worthwhile study'. Even more importantly, there is no prescription of teaching methods, text books or other teaching materials. (However, a recommended list of books that might have been read by 7-year-olds has found its way into the system, showing how easy it would be informally to extend a legally enforceable system once it had been set in place.) The subjects to be taken at GCSE examination are not specified, though, of course, another part of the Act gives the Secretary of State the power to specify which external qualifications may be taken at schools. There had been a general anxiety as to whether the imposition of a national curriculum would stifle curriculum innovation. Section 16 of the Act allows the Secretary of State to lift the requirements of the National Curriculum in the interest of development work and experiments; he or she can only do so on an application by the school's governing body supported by the LEA (or vice versa), or by the National Curriculum Council with the agreement of the LEA and governing body. These formal arrangements were intended to permit formal 'projects'. Circular 5/89 emphasizes that 'Within the framework of attainment targets and programmes of study there will be scope for schools to adopt new approaches without the need for a direction' (para. 50). It is too early to report on the truth of this statement: there have been so many changes to the National Curriculum and assessment arrangements at the government's instance since 1989 that most schools are using what energy they have to maintain adjustments to the formal system.

Finally, the position of pupils with special needs must be clarified. The 1981 Education Act had encouraged their integration into the 'mainstream' of schooling as far as possible and had introduced a formal system of 'statements' for those whose parents wished it and whose handicaps were severe. The government had some difficulty in accommodating statementing and the 'main-streaming' philosophy with the idea of a national curriculum for all. A compromise was reached that will almost certainly not prove stable, and by 1992

The curriculum: the 1980s and after: landmarks

1980   *A Framework for the School Curriculum* (DES);
       A View of the Curriculum (HMI)

1981   *The School Curriculum* (DES); *The Practical Curriculum* (Schools Council)

1982   Technical and Vocational Education Initiative (TVEI)

1983   DES Circular no. 8/83 – enquiry into curriculum arrangements

1985   *Better Schools* – White Paper (DES); *The Curriculum from 5 to 16* (HMI)

1986   Secretary of State announces the intention to introduce a national curriculum

1987   *The National Curriculum 5–16: A Consultation Document*

1987   Task Group on Assessment and Testing (TGAT)

1987   Education Reform Bill presented to Parliament

1988   The Education Reform Act

1989   DES Circular no. 5/89, 'The Education Reform Act; the school curriculum and assessment'

1989   National Curriculum Council (NCC); School Examinations and Assessment Council (SEAC)

---

government was talking of amending the 1981 Act. As things stand (at the time of writing) after the 1988 Act, however, a headteacher may make an exception in respect of the National Curriculum for any pupil for a period of up to six months. Thereafter, if the exception is to continue, the pupil should be assessed by the LEA with a view to making a statement under the 1981 Act. Safeguards are built in, to protect the rights of pupils and parents, and they are strengthened by the fact that some sections of the 1981 Act concerning parents' right of appeal over statementing only came into effect on 1 November 1988.

Overall, probably the greater effect on pupils with problems at school has been through other parts of the policy introduced in 1988, namely the market and competition between schools. Such pupils do not contribute positively to the academic or attendances profile of the school and there is mounting evidence that the number temporarily or permanently excluded from school is increasing. We have therefore returned to the paradox identified earlier, that a national curriculum and a market in schooling are logically incompatible. We have also recited a remarkable cycle in the history of British education, from the Revised Code for Elementary Schools of the nineteenth century, through the inter-war era of enquiry into the fundamentals of curriculum and the liberal philosophy of the 1944 Act, leading to considerable freedom for the individual school, and, in the 1980s, a return to central control in a form more detailed, assertive and comprehensive than ever before.

CHAPTER 6

Appraisal of teachers:
a new policy for the 1990s

APPRAISAL

Another new and still developing aspect of the teachers' working life is 'appraisal'. It must be included in any consideration of the control of education but, as we shall see, it is yet another part of the formal system that is two-edged. No doubt government introduced the requirement for appraisal from a general motive of raising the quality of teaching (some ministers even spoke of getting rid of – 'weeding out' – poor teachers). But also, seen from the viewpoint of an individual teacher, an appropriate appraisal system, faithfully applied in a school, can be an avenue to greater clarity of role, better performance and an improved collegiality, because other teachers are likewise able to improve their performance, and all teachers are given an opportunity to tell 'management' whether its systems – or the lack of them – hinder good classroom or school performance. Appraisal is therefore conspicuously one of those instruments which teachers are well advised to approach positively and with a view to improving their own locus in the network of school relationships, rather than in a spirit of anxiety or a sense that the prime objective will be to create a litany of personal shortcomings. Professional development should be the key objective of a good appraisal system.

Where do things stand at present? It is not possible to be precise, because every LEA or grant-maintained school or city technology college (CTC) is in the process of devising its own scheme. However, there is a history and there are clear national recommendations which set the boundaries and objectives of schemes. They are the product of one of the very few occasions in the 1980s when the DES, LEAs and teachers' associations have been enabled to work constructively together and the outcome has been utilized (albeit selectively) by government – namely the School Teacher Appraisal Pilot Study and its National Steering Group (1987–9).

The recent history of teacher appraisal belongs to the 'accountability movement' of the late 1970s and 1980s. An acceptance of the importance of self-assessment by teachers and schools grew into an insistence by government that employers must 'manage' their teaching force and could do that only if they had 'accurate knowledge of each teacher's performance' (DES, 1983b), and so into a legal requirement that LEAs should appraise their teachers, put into statute in 1986 but not activated until 1991, by which time professional pressure had redirected the main impulse from the punitive and judgemental to support of professional development and school effectiveness. All this constitutes an element of the recent collective experience of teachers and government that has consequences which will not be fully worked out, in the form of completed schemes and programmes of appraisal, until 1994–5. The story is therefore well worth rehearsing in a little more detail for the purposes of this book, where we are trying to understand not only the sinews of formal aspects of control but also their inwardness, so as to empower the teacher.

The appraisal of teachers became an issue in the 1980s. It arose mainly from the desire to improve teaching quality and the need to redeploy teachers between schools as the numbers of pupils fell dramatically throughout the education system. Thus a broad political thrust of policy – 'quality' – was reinforced by a sharp and practical policy requirement. It is often the case that when the practical and urgent reinforce the theoretical and political, something gets done. However, the very nature of these origins also caused hesitant progress at first. Understandably, teachers had no wish to see a crude system of grading put in place for the purposes of performance pay and/or redeployment, still less dismissal from the service. Working on their side were the inherent intricacies and subtleties of assessing an individual professional. Purpose, context, the current state of the art, and much else have to be brought to bear. The politicians and managers, for their part, moved their ground from wanting simple measures that could be directly related to place of employment and pay to accepting that the primary advantage of teacher appraisal would be better-informed decisions by schools, more purposeful in-service training and a secular improvement in teacher performance. It also needs to be borne in mind that discussion of a national policy for appraisal arose before the National Curriculum had made some aspects of the teacher's work more uniform and national conditions of service had clarified other aspects of the teacher's work and working day or year.

The story can usefully start with the DES White Paper of March 1983, *Teaching Quality* (DES, 1983b). Before that, formal systems for teacher appraisal had been very rare in England and Wales, apart from those used for evaluating students during initial teacher training or teachers on probation – all of which were particular to the institution or LEA; no national consensus or body of literature existed. Paragraph 92 of *Teaching Quality* reads:

> The Government welcome recent moves towards self-assessment by schools and teachers, and believe these should help to improve standards and curricula. But employers can manage their teacher force effectively only if they have accurate knowledge of each teacher's performance. The Government believe that for this purpose formal assessment of teacher performance is necessary and should be based on classroom visiting by the teacher's head or head of department, and an appraisal of both pupils' work and of the teacher's contribution to the life of the school. They therefore welcome the interest currently shown among employers and the teachers' associations about the career development and professional assessment of teachers. H.M. Inspectors are collecting evidence about the extent and effectiveness of practices for teacher assessment and self-evaluation in schools, and will make this evidence more widely available. The Government believe that those responsible for managing the school teacher force have a clear responsibility to establish, in consultation with their teachers, a policy for staff development and training based on a systematic assessment of every teacher's performance and related to their policy for the school curriculum.

The emphasis here is on appraisal as a tool of improved management – to help the deployment of teachers and the realization of school development plans through better training.

Two years later, in March 1985, the White Paper *Better Schools* returned to the theme of teacher appraisal and developed it, with a sharper edge (DES, 1985e: para. 180):

> The Government holds to the view expressed in 'Teaching Quality' that the regular and formal appraisal of the performance of all teachers is necessary if LEAs are to have the reliable, comprehensive and up-to-date information necessary for the

systematic and effective provision of professional support and development and the deployment of staff to best advantage. Only if this information relates to performance in post can LEA management make decisions affecting the career development of its teachers fairly and consistently. Taken together, these decisions should result in improved deployment and distribution of the talent within the teaching force, with all teachers being helped to respond to changing demands and to realise their full professional potential by developing their strengths and improving upon their weaknesses; with the most promising and effective being identified for timely promotion; with those encountering professional difficulties being promptly identified for appropriate counselling, guidance and support; and, where such assistance does not restore performance to a satisfactory level, with the teachers concerned being considered for early retirement or dismissal.

The purpose of dismissing unsatisfactory teachers had by now become explicit and salient. Moreover, the emphasis on appraisal as an instrument of management remains clear and the link with performance-related pay is emphasized. For the first time, the concept of a statutory national framework is put forward and legislation to enable the Secretary of State to put it in place is proposed. These paragraphs are so full of the spirit of these times that they bear quoting in full:

181. The Government welcomes the sustained efforts made by many parties to negotiate a new salary structure for primary and secondary teachers, embracing new pay scales, a new contractual definition of teachers' duties and responsibilities and the introduction of systematic performance appraisal, designed to bring about a better relationship between pay, responsibilities and performance, especially teaching performance in the classroom. The appraisal of teacher performance has been widely seen as the key instrument for managing this relationship, with teachers' professional and career development assisted and salary progression largely determined by reference to periodic assessment of performance.

182. It may still be that negotiations across this wide range will prove successful, although the difficulty of reaching an agreement embracing all these elements has always been recognised. Whether or not that is the case, however, the Government believes that the introduction of systematic arrangements for the appraisal of teacher performance, to underpin the improved arrangements for in-service training proposed in paragraphs 175 and 176 and the management of the teacher force, is essential. The Department of Education and Science is in consultation with the local authority and teacher associations to establish what progress can be made in performance appraisal. The Government hopes it may be possible to promote the development of suitable methods and procedures through a project on teacher management and appraisal in a number of LEAs funded with education support grant.

183. The Government believes that consistent arrangements across all LEA areas within a single national framework are needed for a teaching force with a tradition of movement within and across LEA boundaries. This could be achieved through an agreement between the authorities and the teachers' associations. The Government believes, however, that it may prove desirable or even necessary to provide that national framework in the form of statutory regulations, as is already the case for the probation of new teachers. It is proposed therefore that the Secretary of State's existing powers for regulating the employment of teachers should be extended to enable him, in appropriate circumstances, to require LEAs regularly to appraise the performance of their teachers.

The following November (1985), the DES arranged a conference in Birmingham on the theme 'Better Schools, Evaluation and Appraisal'. The Secretary of State, Sir Keith Joseph, returned to teacher appraisal in his address to the conference. His words represent yet another stage in the interplay of interests. He said he hoped that appraisal schemes could be agreed voluntarily, but intended in the meanwhile to take an enabling power. Again, the text (DES, 1986a: 187–8) is worthy of quoting at length:

Closely associated with in-service training, and with the career development of teachers, is the need for LEAs regularly to appraise the performance of their teachers. A sensitively worked out scheme, carefully introduced and embodying adequate safeguards for the individual, would, I am confident, help all teachers realise their full professional potential by providing them with better job satisfaction, more appropriate in-service training and better planned career development.

I repeat that I envisage 'a sensitively worked out scheme, carefully introduced, and embodying safeguards for the individual'. I understand the concern that has been expressed to me about the possibility that annual appraisal procedures might be directly linked to merit pay or annual increments, or be used in other ways by headteachers to give instant rewards or penalties. That is quite definitely not the sort of arrangement I have in mind – nor do I know of any local authority that would wish to use an appraisal scheme in such a way.

But I do believe that the findings from appraisal interviews would lead to better informed promotion decisions by schools and LEAs. This must be an advance on what some of the unions have described as the 'lottery' of the current promotion arrangements, informed as they are by haphazard, informal, unsystematic appraisal of performance. Moreover, I would expect any appraisal scheme to extend to the appraisal of headteachers.

I am often told, too, that a successful appraisal scheme will depend on teachers being properly prepared and trained, and having sufficient time to allocate to the appraisal process. I accept that. The time requirement is one of the considerations to be taken into account in studying the numbers of teachers needed in the longer term. The training requirement could become a priority within the new arrangements envisaged for in-service training. But before we can plan satisfactorily for these developments we need the pilot projects the Department has been seeking to set up.

As you will know, and as foreshadowed in *Better Schools*, the Government plans during this session of Parliament [1985–6] to enable the holder of my office, in appropriate circumstances, to require such appraisal to be carried out. I understand the concern that has been expressed about this, too, along with the view that appraisal systems need to be introduced in co-operation with those who are to be appraised. I agree with that. I therefore stress that what is intended is an enabling power. Whether it will be used will depend upon circumstances. I very much hope that regular teacher-appraisal will be introduced voluntarily – as it can be now by agreement between employer and employee. Considerable effort has been made over a long period in pursuit of an agreement incorporating the introduction of systematic arrangements for appraisal. This effort has sadly not yet borne fruit. Just as sad, I think, is the unwillingness, until now, of the teacher unions to join in with the local authorities and the Department in the preparatory fieldwork which I am sure is necessary if we are to work out a mutually acceptable form of appraisal for teachers. The money set aside by the Government for an ESG [Education Support Grant] in this area remains untouched. But I have not given up hope of practical co-operation in this area, because I am more convinced than ever that appraisal would be a good thing both for standards in the education service and also for the professional development of teachers.

Why does the holder of my office need the proposed power? One reason is that progress in this area has been painfully slow. It may be appropriate to use the new power in association with new arrangements for in-service training to promote more rapid progress. But quite apart from that consideration, it may well be desirable to have a national framework within which local appraisal schemes would operate – after all, the current arrangements for the probation of new teachers are national and this has long been accepted as a means of providing for consistency and fairness. We have no national blueprint to impose. The Government position is that teacher-appraisal should largely be conducted at the level of the individual school by the teachers themselves. It would be done in accordance with general arrangements introduced and monitored by LEAs in accordance with national guidelines worked out in consultation between teachers, employers and the Department. I hope that this conference will mark a new beginning for this co-operative venture.

Next, Section 49 of the 1986 Education (No. 2) Act gave the Secretary of State an enabling power to require LEAs to appraise their teachers, and the protracted negotiations over teachers' pay and conditions, which broke down in virtually all other respects (hence the 1987 Pay and Conditions Act), led to an agreement about pilot schemes of appraisal which would not be linked to pay. The experience of those pilots and the report emanating as a result had a significant influence in the final shape of teacher appraisal. Probably the turning point was the work and report of the Appraisal Training Working Group set up by the Teachers' Dispute ACAS Independent Panel (1986). By that time, the teachers' dispute had been referred to the Advisory, Conciliation and Arbitration Service (ACAS). The pilot schemes themselves were run under the general guidance of the National Steering Group on the School Teacher Appraisal Pilot Study (DES, 1989a). Also of great importance was the parallel report of HMI (DES, 1989b).

The following extract from the 'agreed principles' section of the Report of the ACAS Appraisal Training Working Group (ACAS, 1986) will give a sense of the spirit informing the pilot schemes (quoted Evans and Tomlinson, 1989: 180):

3. Nature and purpose. The Working Group understands appraisal not as a series of perfunctory periodic events, but as a continuous and systematic process intended to help individual teachers with their professional development and career planning, and to help ensure that the in-service training and deployment of teachers matches the complementary needs of individual teachers and the schools. An appraisal system will take into account the following matters:

i) Planning the introduction of EG [entry grade] teachers and assessing their fitness to transfer to an MPG [main professional grade].

ii) Planning the participation of individual teachers in in-service training.

iii) Helping individual teachers, their head teachers and their employers to see when a new or modified assignment would help the professional development of individual teachers and improve their career prospects.

iv) Identifying the potential of teachers for career development, with an eye to their being helped by appropriate in-service training.

v) Recognition of teachers experiencing performance difficulty, the purpose being to provide help through appropriate guidance, counselling and training. Disciplinary procedures would remain quite separate, but might need to draw on relevant information from the appraisal records.

vi) Staff appointment procedures. The relevant elements of appraisal should be available to better inform those charged with the responsibility for providing references.

It will be seen that what the Working Group has in mind is a positive process, intended to raise the quality of education in schools by providing teachers with better job satisfaction, more appropriate in-service training and better planned career development based upon more informed decisions.

The pilot schemes in six LEAs involved the appraisal of 1,690 teachers and 190 headteachers, and the Steering Group Report concluded that the experience gained provided 'a sound basis for the development of appraisal throughout England and Wales'. Commentators at the time could say, 'Once misunderstood, once feared, teacher appraisal is now seen not only as necessary but as the lynch pin of professional development and an issue of central importance to the future progress of the education service' (Evans and Tomlinson, 1989: preface).

The National Steering Group Report recommended that statutory responsibility for securing appraisal should rest with LEAs, but under regulations made by the Secretary of State which would provide a national framework. It proposed a target date of 1994 for full implementation. It also argued that the equivalent of the time of 1,800 teachers would be required if appraisal were to be done properly. This requirement for additional resources seems to have unnerved the DES, and a comical 'on/off' story now ensued. The then Secretary of State, John MacGregor, decided on a further period of consultation and also expressed his concern that bringing forward appraisal at that time would overburden the schools. The regulations expected for the autumn of 1989 were not made.

In September 1990, the Secretary of State announced the result of the national consultation (widespread support for appraisal) and his decision not to lay regulations making appraisal compulsory. His aim instead would be to put in place a national framework which LEAs could implement if they chose. Teachers would have been obliged to participate in such appraisal schemes where introduced. LEAs would also have been empowered to introduce developments of the national framework, but in that case teachers' participation would have been voluntary. The issue of resources would thus have been passed on to the LEAs and schools.

Then there was a change of Secretary of State. Three months later, on 10 December 1990, Kenneth Clarke announced revised plans. He would introduce a national framework and make regulations under Section 49 of the Education (No. 2) Act 1986. So, a period of uncertainty ended with implementation of ideas dating from Sir Keith Joseph's time as Secretary of State, but informed by the collaborative experiences of the pilot schemes. It was also of importance that the Interim Advisory Committee on Teachers' Pay and Conditions continued to urge the introduction of appraisal (see, for example pp. 25-6 of the 4th Chilver Report, 1991). The question of resources was not addressed.

DES Circular no. 12/91 (DES, 1991b) announced that appraisal would be phased in over four years. It was noticeably placatory in tone: 'The Circular is designed to encourage and achieve good practice in schools.' Moreover, it acknowledged the work done earlier: 'It [the Circular] draws on the recommendations of the National Steering Group on School Teacher Appraisal' (para. 3).

Paragraph 4 of the Statutory Regulations of 1991 sets out the aim of appraisal:

Aim of Appraisal

4 (1) Appraising bodies shall secure that appraisal assists –

   (a) school teachers in their professional development and career planning; and
   (b) those responsible for taking decisions about the management of school teachers.

(2) In carrying out their duty under Regulation 3, appraising bodies shall aim to improve the quality of education for pupils, through assisting school teachers to realise their potential and to carry out their duties more effectively.

(3) Appraisal procedures shall in particular aim to –

   (a) recognise the achievements of school teachers and help them to identify ways of improving their skills and performance;
   (b) help school teachers, governing bodies and local education authorities (as the case may be) to determine whether a change of duties would help the professional development of school teachers and improve their career prospects;
   (c) identify the potential of teachers for career development, with the aim of helping them, where possible, through appropriate in-service training;
   (d) help school teachers having difficulties with their performance, through appropriate guidance, counselling and training;
   (e) inform those responsible for providing references for school teachers in relation to appointments;
   (f) improve the management of schools.

The professional development thrust has been preserved. However, there are also elements to do with management, set within certain safeguards, and it remains to be seen how the balance of the effects of appraisal works out in practice.

The six teacher organizations concerned with schools combined to produce a pamphlet in December 1991 which indicates where they think both the advantages and danger points of the government's scheme may lie: *Appraisal: Report of Six Teacher Organisations* (AMA, NAHT, NASUWT, NUT, PAT and SHA). Their views may be summarized as follows:

1 Headteachers have the responsibility to select appraisers. But Circular no. 12/91 says that heads 'should not unreasonably refuse requests from staff for an alternative appraiser if there are particular circumstances which suggest that this might be appropriate'.
2 How information is collected for the purpose of appraisal is governed by a Code of Practice set out as Annex A of Circular no. 12/91. Under this, among other points, the appraiser is required to consult the appraisee on what information will be gathered, and from whom; and appraisers are not expected to consult parents and governors about a teacher.
3 The appraisee should be observed in the classroom on at least two occasions. The teachers' associations observe, 'The appraiser's role is not to be judgmental, but to find a basis for a discussion on the basis of a shared professional experience.'
4 The whole appraisal process must take place within directed time.
5 The appraisal interview should be positive in tone and intention. The Regulations (para. 10.1) state that the interview should include 'reviewing the school teacher's work, identifying the school teacher's achievements and aspects in which further development would be desirable, identifying any training and developmental needs and setting targets for the rest of the appraisal cycle'.
6 It is the appraiser's responsibility to draft the appraisal report. The contents should be discussed and, as far as possible, agreed. Circular no. 12/91 states that 'appraisees are entitled to record their own comments . . . any such comments should form part of the appraisal statement and should be recorded within 20 working days'. Targets should be designed to help, not inhibit, the school teacher and the school has an obligation to support them.
7 Confidentiality has always been a central issue in the discussions about appraisal. The Regulations specify who is

entitled to access to the whole or part of the appraisal statement. In the case of a school teacher, these are:

- the appraisee;
- the appraiser;
- the headteacher (where not the appraiser);
- upon request, the Chief Education Officer (CEO) or any LEA officer/adviser designated by the CEO;
- any review officer following a complaint by the appraisee.

It should be particularly noted that the chair of the governing body is entitled, upon request, to receive any annex to the appraisal statement regarding targets – but not the statement itself. Circular no. 12/91 states at para. 55:

Beyond this, statements should not be disclosed to any persons or body without the consent of the appraisee save in very exceptional circumstances, such as where the statement is relevant and necessary for the fair disposal of legal proceedings or for a police investigation. Legal proceedings means only a Court or Tribunal.

8   Finally, the Regulations also require a complaints procedure and set out certain minimum conditions.

The development of and present requirements for teacher appraisal have been investigated in some detail for two reasons. First, the process will still be developing as new teachers enter the service in the 1990s; it will be therefore unfamiliar to everyone and the new teacher needs access to what reliable information does exist. Second, appraisal is probably the only reform of recent times that will affect every teacher directly. Even the National Curriculum has less relevance for some teachers, say for those mainly teaching 16–19-year-olds. Appraisal is also a process whose results may be used, by the individual and by management, in many different ways. Anxieties about that underlie its history in the 1980s, as we have just seen. It is essential, therefore, that teachers see appraisal as giving them elements of control over their own professional lives and development and do not confer all the power on those organizing and carrying out appraisal. It may prove to be the case that teacher appraisal, first conceived by some as an instrument of general management of 'the teaching force', will become the individual teacher's most valuable source of influence over management.

Appraisal of teachers: a new policy for the 1990s: landmarks

1983	*Teaching Quality* – White Paper
1985	*Better Schools* – White Paper; Sir Keith Joseph's address to conference in Birmingham
1986	Education (No. 2) Act gives the Secretary of State the power to require the appraisal of teachers; Report of the ACAS Appraisal Training Working Group
1987–9	School Teacher Appraisal Pilot Study under National Steering Group (DES, LEAs, teachers)
1990	(September) Secretary of State announces appraisal will not be compulsory
1990	(December) Secretary of State announces appraisal will be compulsory
1991	DES Circular no. 12/91 – appraisal to be phased in over four years; Statutory Regulations issued

CHAPTER 7

In-service training: extended professional development

The changing attitudes of government, LEAs and the teaching profession during the post-war period towards the in-service training of teachers constitute a striking example of the general theme of this book, namely the transition from *laissez-faire* to systematic control, and that control being exercised mainly by central government. It is self-evident that the capacity of the existing body of teachers must be a major determinant, perhaps the major determinant, of the quality of the education system at any time. Yet the first national enquiry into in-service education and training was not mounted until 1970, which seems to suggest that it had broadly been assumed that initial education and training would suffice for a professional lifetime. It is an assumption rooted in a view, perhaps held subconsciously rather than formalized as 'policy', that the task of the teacher remained constant. Like so much in social thinking and policy, that view did not survive the 1960s, as we moved, in Donald Schön's telling phrase, 'Beyond the stable state'. The effects of the social and cultural changes of the 1960s, combined with a broader view of primary education and the desire to provide 'secondary education for all', raised serious questions about the nature of the school curriculum and methods of teaching. (See also Chapter 4.) In consequence, the in-service education and training of teachers became a national issue.

Until that time, it had largely been left to the individual teacher to seek further qualification and to the LEAs, HMIs and higher education institutions to provide courses of training and refreshment according to demand on the one hand and their view of the needs of teachers and the service on the other. The result had been an unsystematic provision of variable quality and geographical accessibility. In some areas rich opportunities were developed and a culture encouraged – not least by the promotions policy pursued by the LEA – in which it was assumed that many teachers would pursue further qualifications and the enrichment of professional skills. In one respect, this *laissez-faire* approach was supported by national policy. The LEAs had agreed with central government to contribute to a national pool of money, 'top-sliced' from the local government block grant before its distribution to the LEAs, which could be drawn upon by an LEA to support teachers who pursued longer courses of study or training. Since each LEA contributed to the national pool in proportion to the number of teachers it employed, there was an inbuilt encouragement to draw from the pool accordingly, and had the system motivated all LEAs roughly equally, there would have been a broad equivalence in the opportunities and encouragement offered to teachers. But in reality, in-service training was not seen as important by all LEAs or by all teachers. Meanwhile central government, in so far as it considered the training of teachers at all, concentrated its attention on the period of initial training (see Chapter 1).

1972–83

We will therefore start the story of policy for in-service education and training (INSET) with the James Report of 1972, because it was the result of the first occasion on which central government had set up an enquiry which included INSET in its brief. The Committee of Inquiry into Teacher Education and Training was set up in 1970, completed its work within a year and published its Report in January 1972 (DES, 1972a). The context of the inquiry is explained in Chapter 1. Considerable changes had occurred in the teaching profession and teacher training since the last restructuring followed the McNair Report of 1944. The school population had expanded dramatically after the war and in consequence the initial training institutions had 120 000 students in them, compared with fewer than 60,000 in 1961. By the end of the 1960s, however, the need for breakneck expansion had eased and, with the prospect of raising the school leaving age to 16 in 1972–3 at last within sight, attention turned to the content, structure and organization of training.

The James Committee took a generous and long-sighted view of the purpose of teaching and betrayed no doubt that its practitioners deserved to be regarded as professionals. It proposed six major objectives, and placed first a large and systematic expansion of in-service training.

In December 1972, the then Secretary of State, Margaret Thatcher, presented a White Paper to Parliament entitled *Education: A Framework for Expansion* (DES, 1972b). It was a considerable state paper and contained imaginative proposals in many aspects of the service from nursery education, schools and teacher training to higher education generally. It carried on the James Committee's view of the purpose of teaching (DES, 1972b: para. 57):

> This goal is no less than building a body of teachers well prepared, academically and professionally, to sustain confidently the formidable task to which they are called: to guide each generation of children into full appreciation of our culture, to enhance their social and moral awareness, to enhance their intellectual abilities to the highest standard of which each is capable, and to develop their practical and human skills so that each may be enabled to make his or her maximum contribution to the health, wealth and harmony of a democratic society.

The White Paper announced that, following consultation, it was clear that the sixfold objectives of the James Committee 'are widely supported. They are fully accepted by the Government' (DES, 1972b: para. 58). It then went on to endorse the Committee's proposals for in-service training – that teachers should be *entitled* to the equivalent of one term in every seven years for INSET. This represents the high-water mark this century of the government's commitment to investing in the teaching profession at work, and paragraphs 60 and 61 are worth quoting in full, since they should not be erased from the folk-memory of teachers:

> 60. The James Committee considered it essential that there be adequate opportunities for the continued education and training of all teachers at intervals throughout their careers. It was therefore their leading and most widely endorsed recommendation that all teachers should be entitled to release for in-service training for periods equivalent to one term in every seven years of service in the first instance. They estimated that actual take-up of such an entitlement would result in 3 per cent of the teaching force being absent on secondment from schools at any one time; this involves a fourfold increase in present opportunity.

> 61. The Government propose to give effect to the Committee's recommendation, in the firm belief that expenditure to achieve an

expansion of in-service training of this order is a necessary invest-
ment in the future quality of the teaching force. The recommendation will need to be implemented over a period as increases in the
teaching force permit larger numbers of teachers to be released.
The raising of the school leaving age will put staffing standards
under temporary strain, but the Government's aim is that a
substantial expansion of in-service training should begin in the
school year 1974–75 and should thereafter continue progressively
so as to reach the target of 3 per cent release by 1981.

Bathos followed: the next year, world oil prices quadrupled
and Britain experienced sharp recession, culminating in 1974 in
the three-day week. The national mood changed dramatically
from support for expansion to concern for economic survival.
As we shall see (Chapters 9 and 10), the agenda for education
had changed dramatically by the mid-1970s. There developed a
new, urgent mood to make education as efficient and effective
as possible and with economic rather than humane objectives
uppermost. None the less, concern for in-service training survived. Its purpose changed, however, to become more specific
and instrumental. Interestingly, and demonstrating the importance attached to it by government, it also became one of
the first territories in which government tried to implement
a policy directly through the LEAs by claiming the right to
make specific grants to LEAs for in-service programmes. Local
government at large, jealous of the principle of the block grant,
resisted the idea and, as we shall see, government at first found
a way round the obstacle, and later introduced legislation to
give it the necessary powers.

We can pick up the story in the Green Paper presented to
Parliament by the then Secretary of State, Shirley Williams, in
July 1977, *Education in Schools: A Consultative Document*
(DES, 1977b). The Green Paper's purpose was to pull together
comment and government's proposals following the 'Great
Debate' on education called for by the Prime Minister, James
Callaghan, in the speech at Ruskin College in October 1976. It
devoted a chapter to teachers and ten substantial paragraphs to
in-service training. The 1972 target of 3 per cent per annum was
not mentioned, but it was stated that expenditure plans
assumed that the number of teachers on induction and in-
service training would rise from the equivalent of 4,500 in 1977
to 18,500 in 1981 (which was roughly 3 per cent of the teaching
force). Some 13,000 places would be available in colleges,
polytechnics and universities to provide courses. The government announced its priorities for INSET, related to specific
objectives and its belief that 'full benefit will only be secured if

in-service training is focused on the specific objectives and problems of individual schools and is therefore to that extent school-based' (DES, 1977b: para. 6.30).

Then came the announcement that the government had found a way to make specific grants for INSET. Funds would be channelled through the Manpower Services Commission (an agency responsible to the Department of Employment) 'for the first year of re-training and, indeed, initial training of teachers of certain shortage subjects'. There was a warning: 'In the longer term, in-service training might be considered appropriate for specific grants' (para. 6.31). We can identify this period as the turning point between a time when INSET was almost entirely left to be pursued by the individual teacher and the present view that it must also, indeed predominantly, serve the needs of the schools and the system as well as the personal or professional development of the individual. That shift of policy gathered pace in the 1980s.

1983–92

In 1983, the Conservative government introduced two developments of long-term importance to in-service training, the White Paper *Teaching Quality* and the Technical and Vocational Education Initiative (TVEI). The first focused, yet again, on the centrality of teachers and therefore their training, and the second, an initiative of the Manpower Services Commission under the auspices of the Department of Employment, further refined the tools of central direction and control.

Teaching Quality (DES, 1983b) explicitly made reference to the earlier Conservative government's *Education: A Framework for Expansion* (DES, 1972b). It stated (DES, 1983b: paras 84, 86):

> The Government adhere to the view expressed in 'Education: A Framework for Expansion', that there is no major profession to which a new entrant, however thorough his initial training, can be expected immediately to make a full contribution . . . a systematic programme of professional initiation and guidance, and further study [is required] . . . As with induction support, so with in-service training: the local education authorities . . . must bear the primary responsibility for providing in-service training – including school-based training – to meet the changing needs of the school system.

The government's expenditure plans by 1984 were to provide

for the release of over 3,000 teachers on courses of varying lengths. (This would have been equivalent to about 1 per cent of school teachers; the 18,000 proposed by Shirley Williams for 1981 – never achieved – would have been about 3 per cent of all teachers; James had proposed 3 per cent.) In *Teaching Quality*, the government also announced its intention to introduce 'a limited scheme of central government grants intended both to increase the total amount of in-service training and also to concentrate part of that training on certain key areas' (DES, 1983: para. 86).

Thus *Teaching Quality* can also be seen as a watershed. The rhetoric that teaching is a major profession is retained from a previous tradition; and the new is ushered in by announcing the mechanism of specific grants and the objective of directed training, which became the two engines by which the government sought to train teachers to deliver the reforms of 1988 and after. The new central systems developed haltingly, however, and with a good deal of inefficiency built in, partly because they were also made to serve a separate and dysfunctional objective, namely a reduction in the power and influence of the LEAs.

1984–92: SPECIFIC GRANTS AND DIRECT CONTROL

In 1984, the Advisory Committee on the Supply and Education of Teachers (ACSET) published its views on the conditions necessary for INSET to be effective. Its proposals took up the themes of professionalism and school focus stated in *Teaching Quality*. Although the committee members did not know it, this was among the last acts of ACSET, because the Secretary of State decided later that year to disband it. The Committee's criteria for effectiveness remain valid and of interest for the context they assume: (ACSET, 1984).

36. For in-service training to be effective, appropriate resources and structures are necessary pre-requisites. Appropriate and adequate resources at school, LEA and provider level are essential for the effective conditions to develop. Teachers should not have to contribute from their own resources towards the cost of INSET activities designed to meet their professional needs identified through the procedures indicated below. Equally important is the provision of suitable structures which will help ensure that INSET is relevant to the needs of teachers and schools, and that optimum use is made of the resources available. Our recommendations for

structures and for funding are dealt with later: this section deals with the conditions which must be satisfied for INSET to be effective.

37. Underlying this section of our report is the recognition that LEAs have a major responsibility to ensure that the needs of individual teachers for INSET are identified and met. As we have indicated, there is a wide spectrum of INSET need and an equally wide spectrum of INSET provision.

The task of matching need with provision is complex but central to the improvement of teaching quality, for which primary responsibility rests with the LEA. We do not believe it is useful to prescribe any single model of INSET: rather we believe it is important at all levels to match particular models of INSET to particular identified needs. As a first step, we have attempted to identify conditions for the effectiveness of INSET.

38. The conditions which the models, the resources and the structures, should satisfy seem to us to be as follows:

(i) identification by teachers of their training needs in relation to the objectives of the school and the LEA, and their own professional development;

(ii) support of Governors, the head teacher and senior staff and local authority advisers and involvement of the whole staff;

(iii) a coherent LEA policy (which should include helping schools and colleges also to develop coherent INSET policies);

(iv) precise targeting of provision;

(v) choice of the appropriate form of INSET, whether individual to the teacher, school based or externally based;

(vi) choice of appropriate length of course and mode of activity;

(vii) relevance to the teachers' need and focused on practice;

(viii) appropriate expertise on the part of higher education institutions and other providers of INSET;

(ix) appropriate preparatory and follow-up work in schools.

Teaching Quality (1983), ACSET (1984) and *Better Schools* (1985) were all concerned with the problems facing a government that wished to implement changes in schooling and therefore wanted teachers to adopt new objectives and methods. There were regional disparities of INSET. Priorities differed between LEAs because they reflected local perceptions and traditions and because funding was contained within the central government rate support grant and not earmarked specifically for INSET. There was also a lack of any overall control. Except for the specific powers conferred by the Education (Grants and Awards) Act 1984, the DES possessed until 1987 only indirect control of funding through 'the pool' – from which LEAs were reimbursed the fees of teachers who attended approved courses of more than 60 days. This implicit promotion of long courses (the pool was 'open', not 'capped') had important policy consequences. It encouraged the location of INSET in institutions for extended periods of study away from the day-to-day concerns of the school. It had been the chief avenue by which the ambitious individual had gained higher qualifications: and its effects had not been monitored through either research or policy-led enquiries.

The Technical and Vocational Education Initiative (TVEI), by contrast, provided funding to LEAs and schools on the basis of a contract, pre-set criteria and monitoring of results. It quickly spawned a scheme of in-service training (TRIST, TVEI-related in-service training). The origins and development of TRIST have been traced in Merson (1989) and the broader movements of government INSET policy and funding 1983–90 have been analysed by Goodyear (1992). Goodyear argues, 'In essence, TRIST in 1985–86, under the MSC, incorporated much DES thinking, as set out in *Better Schools* . . . , on ways of developing INSET policy so as to overcome its previous inconsistency and relative ineffectiveness in practice' (1992: 4). It quickly became clear that the DES was determined to follow the specific grant model as adopted in TRIST, because before the results of any evaluation of TRIST were made known, and before it had been running a full year, the DES launched the Local Education Authority Training Grants Scheme (LEATGS) in Circular no. 6/86 (DES, 1986b) and subsequently in regulations made under the Education (No. 2) Act 1986. The aims of LEATGS, set out in Circular no. 6/86, mention professional development but then change the language: 'systematic . . . planning . . . to encourage . . . effective management . . . training to meet . . . needs . . . accorded national priority' (para. 4; see also Goodyear, 1992: 6).

The model was taken from TRIST: bids against criteria, and earmarked grant and monitoring, especially in order to ensure 'contract compliance'. LEATGS ran in parallel with Education Support Grants (ESG), introduced in 1985 under the Education (Grants and Awards) Act 1984, to promote innovation wanted by the government. The two systems were not integrated or synchronized over the year, so that they proved cumbersome and time-consuming for the LEAs. There was obviously room for rationalization and in 1990 Grants for Educational Support and Training (GEST), a new programme of DES grants for INSET, attempted to co-ordinate the two systems while keeping them separately identifiable. At the same time, the concept of LEAs bidding for grants for local priorities disappeared and they became solely an instrument of central government policy. The Secretary of State's declared objectives for GEST were:

> To target as much support as possible on:
> - implementing the Education Reform Act (ERA), including the in-service training needed to ensure that teachers are properly prepared for the reforms
> and
> - improving teacher recruitment.

Several conclusions and at least one paradox may be drawn from the development of government policy for INSET between 1986 and 1992. On the one hand, there is a clear trend towards central control. A study of the four LEATGS circulars of 1986–9 reveals a steady increase in the demand by DES for more and more detailed information from LEAs and therefore closer involvement and control. The place of training in the introduction of an increasingly detailed national curriculum was firmly established by Circular no. 5/88 (DES, 1988c) which made it a first priority and gave it an explanatory annex of its own. As Goodyear points out (1992: 14):

> It is exactly the kind of shift predicted by Janet Harland in her article of 1987: 'The New INSET: A Transformation Scene', where she argues that specific grant funding leads to 'a conception of curriculum control and development as something logically prior to teacher development'.

This trend runs counter to the tradition of the teacher as autonomous professional and suggests a more limited, functionary status. It was reinforced by the virtual removal of grants for local priorities. In 1991, the only head under which LEAs could get support for any locally determined initiative was 'Activity 24', which was only 10 per cent of total supported expenditure and such a rag-bag of disparate activities that no strong initiative could be based upon it. To this extent, the introduction and development of specific grants for INSET involved a reduction in LEA autonomy over initiatives and an increasing use of LEAs as local agencies of DES policy (see also Chapter 9), combined with a redefinition of the teacher as functionary.

But, as Goodyear argues, there was another strand of INSET in the same period which represented a countervailing force because it required both LEA initiative and teacher professionalism: hence the paradox. Much of the ESG-supported

INSET involved a series of National Curriculum-driven projects which were classroom- and competency-centred. Such projects relied on the skills of good practitioners, recruited, trained and seconded by LEAs as advisory teachers to disseminate their skills directly and practically in primary schools. Annex A of Circular no. 5/88 encouraged LEAs to use Education Support Grants to complement training, and states that 'teachers are to be supported and trained by advisory teachers appointed under the ESG scheme'. Circular no. 20/89 (DES, 1989e) carried this policy forward and it survived into the reformed system, GEST, in 1990, but rapidly declined in importance and influence after that time.

INSET: THE POSITION IN THE EARLY 1990s

Where are we now? *At the level of policy-making*, the power has been drawn strongly into the centre. It is there that priorities for INSET are decided. What is left to LEAs and schools and institutions within such a policy is a subsidiary role of identifying where applications of policy are needed – because of a shortfall in skills, the arrival of new staff, or a reorganized school, for example. This central power is reinforced by the mechanisms. The apparatus of DES-determined criteria, detailed guidance for bidding by LEAs and monitoring for cost-effectiveness all reduce those in LEAs and schools to agents working on an externally determined agenda.

The same analysis could be applied to the status conferred on the teachers. To the extent that the education system does not produce what government requires, it is because the teachers fail to 'deliver'. They must therefore be retooled and retrained so that they *can* 'deliver' (a revealing term in itself). It was stated explicitly in Circular no. 20/89 (DES, 1989e) that the Secretary of State's main aim is

> to ensure that teachers and other professional groups involved are sufficiently well-trained to secure the effective introduction and implementation of the government's policies to improve the quality of education (para. 4).

It is the experience of those working in higher education that, during the period this policy has been developing, fewer and fewer teachers have found time or money to undertake general courses for higher qualifications. It remains likely, however, that just as the successes achieved by teachers in introducing the National Curriculum were based on their general training and professionalism, so the longer-term capacity of teachers to manage change will be reduced if the only training they are to receive is directed towards immediate and specific ends.

What we have seen since 1983 is an assertion by government of policies for INSET that it believes will raise standards in education, and a directed training of teachers to that end. Such central control and standardization are understandable in that context. But it would be disingenuous to pretend that means do not affect ends. The question is whether the policy will not soon involve a self-defeating cost in quality if the possibility of local initiatives and experiment by teachers continues to be curtailed.

At the level of the individual school and for the individual teacher, these mechanisms of control will not be apparent in exactly the form described in this chapter. The school will have its development plan, its system for appraising teachers, its information about assessment of pupils at Key Stages and otherwise; and from all this it will devise plans for INSET, and the individual teacher will feel more or less committed to and supportive of those plans depending on the management style of the school and how far it functions as a collegial unity. But as a teacher, you will need also to have a care for your own INSET. Only you can form ideas about your need for further personal development, whether it takes the form of academic study, professional and pedagogical enquiries, or general skills such as counselling or appraisal. You will probably feel the need for some or all of these at different times. The tide is beginning to turn against placing so much emphasis on the school's assessment of its own needs and certainly against trying to meet them from its own resources: that way, inadequacies may be recycled or reinforced and needs not always fully understood. The importance of an external view and assistance from beyond the school itself is being increasingly understood and accepted, although the funding mechanisms may take some years to catch up. You will find allies within and beyond the school, in teachers' associations which provide valuable INSET, and in universities and colleges where initial training, scholarship and research maintain a lively view of education. Now you know something of the recent history of INSET, you will be better able to think out your own position and argue your case.

End note

In December 1992, OFSTED (the Office for Standards in Education) announced that HMI would no longer run short courses for teachers, thus ending the tradition of a hundred and fifty years and severing the national inspectorate from feeding into the professional development of teachers. No explanation was offered. The announcement was undated and not signed.

In-service training: extended professional development: landmarks

1972	James Report
1972	*Education: A Framework for Expansion* – White Paper
1976	Ruskin Speech and Great Debate
1977	*Education in Schools: A Consultative Document* – Green Paper; government grants for INSET for first time, via Manpower Services Commission
1983	*Teaching Quality* – White Paper
1983	Technical and Vocational Education Initiative (TVEI)
1983	TRIST (TVEI-related in-service training)
1984	Report of Advisory Committee on the Supply and Education of Teachers (ACSET)
1984	Education (Grants and Awards) Act Empowered Secretary of State to make specific grants
1985	*Better Schools* – White Paper
1986	DES Circular no. 6/86
1986	Local Education Authority Training Grants Scheme (LEATGS)
1986	Education (No. 2) Act
1988	DES Circular no. 5/88
1989	DES Circular no. 20/89
1990	Grants for Educational Support and Training (GEST)

CHAPTER 8

School governors

You will have realized by now that the members of the school governing body have considerable influence in and on the school. It was they who gave you your appointment, and they have the power of dismissal. They are also responsible for the general conduct of the school. They are a mixture of teachers, parents, community members and LEA appointees in roughly equal parts. The headteacher is always a governor. So what is the purpose lying behind the idea of putting a group of both lay and professional people in this relationship to a school, and how does it bear on our theme of control? In particular, how will you, as a teacher at the school, come across from time to time the powers or influence of the governing body?

The story of how government has brought governors into greater prominence since the 1970s is an interesting one. It contains many elements directly connected with our theme of control: bringing parents into greater prominence; increasing the accountability of the school to its immediate community, as well as formally to the LEA and DES; delegating greater responsibility for finance and management to the school; centring on the school responsibility for 'delivering' the National Curriculum; and lastly, making the school the 'unit of exchange' in the educational market place – that is, the focus of parents' choice on behalf of their children. In short, during the 1970s and 1980s the school has been made the engine of policy delivery and accountable for its success or failure. In this process, the governing body has become the politically constituted responsible body. Yet none of its members can be held individually accountable for financial loss or other mistakes; the governors may delegate all or some of their duties to the headteacher; and while governors serve only a four-year term (which is renewable), the teachers are likely to have longer-term contracts and see the school's work and reputation in a longer perspective. As the 1990s unfold, the role of the governors and their relationships with the teachers and the LEA (or the DES in the case of a grant-maintained school) are still being worked through for the first time on the basis of the legal settlements now in force. It is therefore even more necessary to understand the recent history and underlying purposes.

The 1870 Education Act had permitted school boards to delegate some of their powers to the managers of elementary schools. Since 1902, when LEAs were set up, school managers (for primary schools) and governors (for secondary schools) have had local responsibility for the welfare and progress of individual schools. Their antecedents were the governors first introduced in the early nineteenth century to inspect those schools in receipt of government grants, set up by the National Society and the British and Foreign Schools Society.

In this they were following a still older tradition, probably established by William Wykeham when he founded Winchester School in 1382. He provided for 'an external assessment of the work of the school and of its food'. Every year between 7 July and 1 October, the Warden of New College and two of the 'discreeter' Fellows were, at the cost of that College, to go to Winchester 'with no more than six horses' and there (Leach, *Educational Charters: Statutes of New College, Oxford*, quoted DES, 1977a: 143):

> diligently inquire and hold a scrutiny on the government of the Warden of the same college and the master teacher in grammar, the ushers under him, and the scholars and other persons living in the same college, and the quality of the food provided for the same, and other articles contained in the Statues [*sic*] of the college at Winchester; and shall correct and reform anything needing correction or reform.

The 1944 Education Act further increased the powers and duties of governors and required each school to have a managing or governing body. This intention was frustrated in many areas, especially towns, where schools were grouped together and either shared one set of governors or were controlled by a sub-committee of the Education Committee, acting as governing body from time to time. The 1944 Act had not intended the let-out clause to be used to such an extent. As a result, therefore, of the professional salience of the headteacher and the political approach of some LEAs, governors in some areas became little more than either the 'dignified' part of the school's constitution or a rubber stamp for the decisions of the LEA. It was not so everywhere. In some LEAs, notably counties which for practical and historical reasons had a more devolutionary frame of mind, governors were given real authority. In some they appointed staff, including the headteacher, with only a reserve power taken by the LEA to disapprove; in others the governors were made the trustees of the school's buildings and of its reputation in the community, on behalf of an LEA which regarded them as its local arm.

Nevertheless, the predominant picture was of a system fallen into desuetude. A research study carried out between 1965 and 1969 (Baron and Howell, 1974) showed that of the 78 county boroughs in England only 21 had set up governing bodies for each of their schools, and that in 20 the council simply nominated a single governing body to act for all its schools. Of the 45 counties, 22 had set up individual governing bodies. Having reviewed this and other evidence, the Committee of Inquiry chaired by Taylor (appointed in 1975) concluded (DES, 1977a: para. 2.9):

> there was little evidence to show that, at the time of the study, the standard provision in the articles that 'the governors shall have the general direction of the conduct and curriculum of the school' was taken seriously. Heads invariably maintained that they were entirely responsible for deciding what was taught, although they kept governors informed of any change of note. Similarly, the most frequent response from governors was that they felt that the curriculum should be left to the head and his staff. There were instances, however, of reports being made by heads of departments or other teachers on aspects of teaching in the school.

It is important to remember that while the Taylor Committee was sitting, James Callaghan made the Ruskin College speech, which advocated a core curriculum and a stronger role for parents and governors. The anxieties about the weakness of governing bodies reflected other anxieties about the curriculum, and the relative weakness of parents and other 'stakeholders' compared with teachers. The growing interest in strengthening governing bodies, apparent from the mid-1970s onwards, had its roots in these twin concerns. There was also another cause, connected with the power that had accreted to the LEAs and the teachers. It concerned the 'politicization' of

121

education. This is a vast theme, and it will be more usefully dealt with in Chapters 9 and 10, which review and analyse broad policy. But to understand the move towards encouraging more prominence for governors, it should be borne in mind that the change to comprehensive education had by this time (the mid-1970s) become a party political issue, and there were also worries that some teachers might abuse the freedom given them over the curriculum. This second concern also cropped up in a pathological form in a primary school just before and during the deliberations of the Taylor Committee. It was the so-called Tyndale School Affair, which led to a public enquiry and a report by Robin Auld QC in 1976 (ILEA, 1976).

Tyndale Junior School had 217 pupils on roll when a new headteacher assumed office in the autumn term of 1973. He began a process of bringing the whole staff (five, including himself) into discussions about educational aims and teaching methods. But the attempt only revealed sharp divisions about educational aims and teaching methods, so that (ILEA, 1976: paras 188-9):

> each teacher continued as before to follow his or her own individual teaching and disciplinary methods . . . Not only did the staff meetings fail to produce any distinct educational policy as to the school's aims and teaching methods upon which the whole staff could agree, but they soured staff relations and affected the daily running of the school.

From this beginning, which in many other circumstances and with different *personae dramatis* would have been resolved constructively, there ensued a two-year period in which the school virtually broke down as a working organization and also attracted to it external pressures, actions and failures of both a political and professional kind, so that the LEA decided upon a public inquiry. In all this, the role of the school managers was prominent, though by no means always unhelpful. The details are recounted fully in the Auld Report (ILEA, 1976). The essential lesson was that it was possible, given an exceptional set of internal and external circumstances, that a school could fall apart so far as teaching and discipline were concerned and become a centre of political intrigue and accusations of conspiracy. The role of the managers, and the blurred nature of their responsibilities, the action or inaction of the authority's inspectorate and administration, and the impact upon pupils and parents and the associated Infants School were all considered by Auld. His Report did not place the government of education as it impinged on an individual school in a favourable light.

The Taylor Committee therefore worked within a context where it was generally expected that something radical would be recommended, and not before time. The Report admits that to retain the existing arrangements for governing bodies was not an option: 'the effective choice lay between reforming, replacing and abolishing them' (DES, 1977a: para. 3.3).

There is a striking essay on the history of school governance, 597–1945, in the Taylor Report which is worth reading for its own sake at any time. It shows how the public authorities for education, as they were set up and given greater responsibilities from the nineteenth century on, tended to take an increasing control over schools, to the detriment of the powers of governors. The writer continues (DES, 1977a: 183):

> To-day when the responsible public authorities are fewer in number [following the reform of local government in 1974] and, it is said, more 'remote', when the teachers are no longer the 'poor ushers' of by-gone days when, largely as a result of the reforms of 1944, there is a much larger body of better educated and articulate parents, many of them anxious to 'participate' and when, in terms both of beliefs and ethnic origins, the nation is of a more heterogeneous character than it has been for a very long time, other voices are to be heard claiming that they too should have a share in this control.

The issues being examined by the Taylor Committee, which essentially amounted to the debate which recurs in every generation, 'To whom *do* schools belong?' (the title of a book by Lester Smith published in 1942, for example), taking place in the context it did could lead to only one recommendation: governing bodies should be reformed in order to increase the constituency of stake-holders in education and should be given more power – including the assertion of those powers over curriculum and conduct which had existed but lain neglected.

The Taylor Committee recommended that every school should have its own governing body (the term 'managers' was to be dropped). The governors should see themselves as part of a continuum of government from LEA to headteacher. Four groups should be equally represented: the LEA, the school staff, the parents and the local community. The powers and duties of governors were also examined, and the report recommended ways in which responsibility for the curriculum, finance, the school premises, staff appointments, and the admission, supervision or expulsion of pupils was to be divided between governors and LEA.

But unanimity was not reached on all points. The report also contains a note of extension by seven members (nearly one-third), a note of dissent by another member and a minority report and letter to the chairman by yet another (who refused to sign the Report). The note of extension is particularly interesting in view of later developments. It suggested that parents should have the legal rights to be given information about the school their child attended or intended to attend, to consultations with teachers, and of access to information about their child's education. This was a claim on behalf of individual parents, their collective rights having been provided for in the main report. The claim to an individual right was based on a persuasive argument, namely that the law placed responsibility for securing the child's education upon the parent(s) (DES, 1977a: 121):

> We therefore ask the Secretaries of State to consider giving each individual parent the right in law to the information relevant to the performance of his legal duty . . . We should like to emphasise that this request represents no threat to the individual teacher or to the orderly running of schools. We do not intend that a parent should have access to classrooms, teachers or written material except in accordance with arrangements made by the school and approved by the governors . . . In the long run the well-informed parent is the best protection and support for the work of the school.

The controversy that had been evident in the Committee's debates also greeted the Report. Some LEAs did not like the concept of four equal partners, the extension of governors' powers was regarded with suspicion by both LEAs and teachers, and the National Union of Teachers (NUT) called the Report 'a busybody's Charter'. However, there was general support for doing something.

Shirley Williams, the then Secretary of State, therefore decided to deal separately with the two issues of composition and powers. The Education Bill published in 1978 contained five clauses on school government. It proposed that all schools should have governing bodies. The composition would be determined by national regulation, but would include parents, teachers and, for county secondary schools, the local community and pupil governors over the age of 16. At the same time a White Paper, *The Composition of Governing Bodies* (DES, 1978b) made detailed proposals for what would be set out in the regulations, but did not include the powers of governors.

The Bill fell as a result of the change of government in 1979. The new government quickly published a Bill that was to become the Education Act 1980. It included five clauses which were very similar to those in the 1978 Bill; but it also contained sections on school admissions and parental preferences, both issues that had been discussed in the Taylor Report.

A primary purpose of the 1980 Act, one of the four major pieces of education legislation put in place by Conservative governments between 1979 and 1988, was to give parents more choice over the school their child could attend. It was the first step in creating a 'market' in schooling. The reform of governing bodies, carried over from the previous government and the Taylor Report, was made mainly to support parental choice and to increase the local accountability of schools. The 1980 Act ruled that each school should have its own governing body, unless the LEA considered that two schools could share a governing body. It laid down that there must be parent and teacher governors, but did not radically alter the composition of governing bodies. There was no reference in the Act to the powers of the governing body. Many sections of the Act were not legally required until 1 September 1985, although in the event a number of LEAs brought in the changes before that.

The next big step in reforming governors came in 1986, and by that time the context, once again, had changed radically. The Education (No. 2) Act 1986 went through Parliament at a time when schools and LEAs were in turmoil as a result of the prolonged dispute over teachers' pay and conditions of service. The Act profoundly affected the control of schools and what was taught in them. It was the result of the development of government policy over three or four years. It brought together issues of parental choice, parental involvement in schools, and clarification of the purposes of schooling – all in a context where the powers of LEAs had been subtly eroded by financial restriction and transfer of responsibility to the DES or schools. It will be helpful, therefore, to look at the threads that run through two state papers, *Parental Influence at School* (May 1984) and *Better Schools* (March 1985). They form the public crucibles for the ideas of the 1986 Act; the elements which they melded had been mined from two separate ores: Conservative political philosophy, and ideas developed within the educational world during the previous ten years.

Parental Influence at School: A New Framework for School

Government in England and Wales was a government consultative paper (DES, 1984b) which claimed lineage from the
Taylor Report. It proposed to give parents 'elected by their
fellow parents' the right to form a majority of the governing
body and to define clearly and increase the functions of the
governing body, 'so that they can co-operate effectively with
LEAs, heads and other teachers in promoting good education'
(para. 3). It thus went well beyond the Taylor recommendation
for equality of representation among four constituencies, and
proposed to clear up the question of functions (that is, power
and control). The Green Paper itself spoke only of defining
'clearly' the functions: the accompanying press notice stated
that the aim was 'to define clearly and increase the functions of
governing bodies in relation to those of local education
authorities and headteachers' (DES, 1984c). The existing position over functions was described as 'confusing, unsatisfactory
for parents and teachers, and harmful to good education': most
governing bodies 'do not adequately serve the aim of promoting
the school as a force for good in the life of the pupils, their
families and the community which it serves . . . the proposals
complement the Government's policies for the school curriculum, examinations and teaching quality' (press notice).

It can be seen how curriculum, assessment, the quality of
teaching, value for money and parental influence were all
beginning to be focused upon the school: the reform of school
governance was a prerequisite. Every dominant theme of the
second half of the 1980s was played for the first time, though
often in a minor key:

- *Curriculum*: the governors would have a duty to determine
  the statement of the school's curricular aims and would call
  for reports from the headteacher.
- *Conduct* of the school would be under the governors'
  general control – that is, school rules, relationships within
  school and with the outside world, and the representation
  of the school to the outside world.
- *Discipline*: the governors would have status in matters of
  discipline, including the suspension of pupils.
- *Appointment of staff* would be made by panels in which
  LEA and governors were equally represented.
- *Finance*: The LEA would have a duty to provide the governors annually with an itemized statement of recurrent
  expenditure, so that they could 'form a judgement on
  whether that expenditure was providing value for money'.

This clause was especially redolent of future developments. Within four years, the government moved from giving governors a retrospective duty to check the value for money to giving them responsibility for managing a delegated budget.

- *Governors' annual report and parents' meeting*: the idea for these first appears.

To those particularly concerned with managing the service as a whole, the proposed devolution of power to governors and consequent fragmentation of management was not wholly attractive. An internal paper of the Association of County Councils (ACC) echoed the views of LEAs generally and also the fears of teachers that their proper professional role might be reduced:

> The Green Paper does not contribute very usefully to the development of better management practice in the maintained Education Service. It is not possible easily, if at all, to see in what ways the Green Paper proposals would help LEAs to manage falling rolls, make more effective and efficient use of reducing resources, establish agreed measures to assess teacher performance, or promote 'effectiveness, efficiency and economy' in accordance with the Audit Commission's new requirements.

The ACC paper was not negative about other government initiatives. It went on:

> This lack of relevance of the Green Paper's proposals sharply contrasts with the great practical value of the policy developments set out in Circulars 6/81 and 8/83 concerning the school curriculum. The sensible policies set out in the White Paper 'Teaching Quality' are also not properly reflected in the Green Paper.

The Green Paper *Parental Influence at School* did not lead directly to legislation; there was an intermediate stage in which the government's policies for education were gathered more robustly together, and which culminated in the White Paper of March 1985, *Better Schools*. This was the last considerable state paper of the Conservative government of the 1980s before it entered its radical phase and introduced a National Curriculum and a wholehearted market-value approach to schooling. It is therefore of great interest for the general development of policy. This aspect is considered in Chapter 10. So far as school governors were concerned, *Better Schools* tackled the issue from two angles: indirectly through policies on parental involvement in schools, and directly by proposing reform of governing bodies.

Chapter 7 of *Better Schools* was entitled 'Parents and schools'. It drew together two contrasting threads and thereby acknowledged explicitly, perhaps for the first time in a government paper since 1979, that parents were not only 'consumers' (the parental choice thrust of policy) but also educators (and should therefore be encouraged to think of the schools as partners) (DES, 1985e: para. 196):

> The 1980 Act gave parents a greater say in the activities of maintained schools by allowing parents of pupils at a school to elect one or two members of the governing body . . . the government now intends further to increase parental influence at school through measures relating to school government.

The next paragraph, however, began, 'The child's education begins at home. It is in the family that personal and social development begins and a start is made on many of the skills, for example in language, which the schools develop', and went on 'at school . . . parent and school become partners in a shared task for the benefit of the child' (para. 197). The paper goes on to encourage schools and parents to find more and better ways to share information and co-operate in activities. Outreach schemes were commended in which teachers, especially from nursery and primary schools, visited homes and the interest of parents was first engaged.

The tone and language of Chapter 7 suggest an attempt to combine the assertiveness of the parental role in choosing and helping govern schools with the humility required of both parent and teacher when they work together as educators. The awkwardnesses and incompatibilities of the policies asserted after 1988 lie latent but clearly visible in this part of *Better Schools*, and the attempt is made to reconcile – or nullify – them by an appeal to the parents' and teachers' common interest in the benefit of the child, once the point of choice of school is passed. It marks the high tide in the 1980s of an acknowledgement that partners and competitive consumers are awkward bedfellows. It was not to last.

We may now turn to the proposals in *Better Schools* for reforming school government. They were predicated on an important idea which belonged to a deep tradition in the education service, and one that had been strengthened by research and experience since the 1960s: namely, that a school is more successful if it is capable of thinking for itself and succeeds in operating as a whole entity with an identity and purpose of its own. Moreover, the school is made still more effective if it is connected to its local community. Again, these are broad and rich themes of policy development which will be set in that context in Chapters 9 and 10. For the moment, it is important to note that the government made them the rationale for its reform of government bodies (DES, 1985e: para. 215):

> If a school is to succeed in all its tasks, it needs to have an identity and a sense of purpose of its own. It needs to recognise itself as more than an agency of the LEA. While the professionalism of its staff is a necessary condition for its success, it is not sufficient on its own. A school should serve the community from which it draws its pupils. To facilitate all these aims county, maintained special, and controlled schools have been required by the Education Acts to have governing bodies which were intended to introduce a lay element into the conduct of their affairs.

The government had identified three obstacles to 'realising the full potential of governing bodies as a force for good in the life of individual . . . schools'. First, insufficient account was taken of 'parents' natural and special interest in their children's education and progress'; second, the powers of governors were too restricted in relation to those of the LEA and the headteacher; third, LEAs had the power '(of which they usually avail themselves)' to appoint a majority of governors (para. 217).

As to composition, the government proposed that no single interest should predominate. This was an important change from the dominant role suggested for parents in the Green Paper a year earlier. The scheme proposed was as shown in its table of 'The proposed composition of governing bodies' (see overleaf) (DES, 1985e: 65).

As to powers, the government's aim, Sir Keith Joseph told the House of Commons on 26 March 1985, was 'to entrench the powers of governing bodies of county, controlled and maintained special schools in relation to the functions of the LEA and the headteacher' (DES, 1985b).

Chapter 9 of *Better Schools*, 'The legal framework', is fifty-one paragraphs long and deals solely with the reform of governing bodies. These proposals were now projected forward into the Education (No. 2) Act of 1986, which set into statute the current basis of the powers and constitution of governing bodies.

The proposed composition of governing bodies for county, voluntary controlled and maintained special schools

Size of school	Elected by and from parents[b]	Appointed by LEA	Head-teacher[c]	Elected by and from teachers	Co-opted[d] or, for controlled schools: Foundation		Co-opted[d]	Total
Fewer than 100 pupils	2	2	1	1	2	3	1	9
100–299 pupils	3	3	1	1	3	4	1	12
300 pupils or more[a]	4	4	1	2	4	5	1	16
600 pupils or more[a]	5	5	1	2	4	6	2	19

Notes: (a) The LEA would be free to choose either composition for schools with 600 or more pupils.

(b) Where insufficient parents stood for election (or, in any case, for schools with at least 50 per cent boarders) the LEA would appoint parent proxies to fill vacancies. LEA members and employees and co-opted members of the Education Committee would be ineligible for such proxy appointments.

(c) The headteacher would be able to choose not to be a governor.

(d) The number of co-optees would be reduced by one to allow for the addition shown in the following mutually exclusive circumstances: –

   (i) one representative of the minor authority (or minor authorities, acting jointly) in the case of a county or controlled primary school serving an area in which there is one or more minor authorities;

   (ii) one representative of the District Health Authority in the case of a hospital special school;

   (iii) one representative of a relevant voluntary organisation in the case of any other maintained special school.

THE EDUCATION (NO. 2) ACT 1986

In summary, the Act distributed places on the governing body almost equally between parents, LEA, teaching staff and local community. The general responsibility for the conduct of the school was placed with the governors. The school curriculum was to be agreed between LEA, governors and headteacher by a procedure laid down, and parents were to be kept informed, also by due procedure.

There were detailed procedures over the discipline of pupils, including suspensions and exclusions from school. A budget for books, equipment and stationery was to be delegated by the LEA and controlled by the governors. And the governors were to hold an annual meeting of parents and present an annual report on their stewardship. Provided the meeting was quorate (at least 20 per cent of eligible parents present), it could pass resolutions concerning the school, the governors and the LEA. There were detailed instructions on how staff, including the headteacher, were to be appointed, with elements of power being transferred from LEA to governors.

At last, the long travail since the mid-1970s over the distribution of powers between LEA, governors and headteacher seemed to have been settled. The notion of the school governing body as a crucial part of the government of education had triumphed. Its new powers and functions were such that it could be described as one of the 'new magistracies' called into being during the 1980s (see Chapters 9 and 10). These powers were soon to be both changed and extended still further by the Education Reform Act 1988, but the framework set up in 1986 remains the basis of school government, and any teacher needs to understand it thoroughly. For details, you must consult the Act itself and specialist handbooks, but the following is a working guide.

Composition of Governing Bodies as set down in the Education (No. 2) Act 1986

School Governors: A New Role defines the composition of governing bodies as follows (DES, 1988a):

County and voluntary controlled schools

Up to 99 Pupils	100–299 pupils
2 parents	3 parents
2 LEA appointees	3 LEA appointees
1 teacher	1 teacher
3 co-optees	4 co-optees
(or 1 co-optee +	(or 1 co-optee +
2 foundation at	3 foundation at
controlled schools)	controlled schools)
1 headteacher	1 headteacher
(if head so chooses)	(if head so chooses)
300–599 pupils	600 + pupils*
4 parents	5 parents

4 LEA appointees	5 LEA appointees
2 teachers	2 teachers
5 co-optees	6 co-optees
(or 1 co-optee +	(or 2 co-optees +
4 foundation at	4 foundation at
controlled schools)	controlled schools)
1 headteacher	1 headteacher
(if head so chooses)	(if head so chooses)

* these schools have the option of adopting the composition specified for schools of 300–599 pupils.

Voluntary aided and special agreement schools

The composition of the governing bodies of these schools was not changed by the Act. The non-foundation governors must comprise:

- at least one parent

- at least one LEA appointee

- at least one teacher for schools with 299 or fewer pupils and at least two teachers for larger schools

- at least one minor authority appointee at primary schools serving an area with a minor authority

- the headteacher if he or she so chooses and there must be sufficient foundation governors (one of whom must be a parent) to outnumber the others by two if the governing body has 18 or fewer members and by three if it is larger.

These new arrangements were implemented by September 1988 for county schools and September 1989 for controlled schools. Aided schools were virtually unaffected so far as composition was concerned.

The Act said that no governors under the age of 18 could serve, finally removing the possibility of pupil governors as recommended in the Taylor Report. Governors would serve a four-year term, but LEAs retained the power under Section 21(c) of the 1944 Education Act to remove governors they had appointed. However, an Appeal Court decision of 1989 (*Regina* v. *Inner London Education Authority* ex parte *Brunyate and Hunt*) apparently curtailed that power by ruling that governors had a right to exercise their powers within an independent sphere of responsibility, as intended by the 1944 Act. The two governors concerned had refused to follow the ILEA policy line on whether the voluntary-aided school, Haberdashers' Aske's, should seek grant-maintained or CTC status. It was not surprising, therefore, that a month later the Court of Appeal found against the Westminster Roman Catholic Archdiocesan education authority in removing governors who had refused to support a scheme of tertiary organization proposed by the (Archdiocesan) School Trustees. In this case, Lord Justice Glideswell found that 'the control of the characteristics of the school and the nature of the education provided was a matter exclusively for the governors' (*Regina* v. *Westminster Roman Catholic Diocese Trustee* ex parte *Andrews* (1989): Law Report, *The Independent*, 27 July 1989). Although both these cases concerned voluntary-aided schools, the general view is that the Education (No. 2) Act 1986 removed any important distinction between county and voluntary schools in these respects. It suggests that school governors generally are in a strong position, once appointed, and have an overriding duty to consider the interests of the individual school rather than any extraneous circumstances. This is particularly significant since many services and functions, such as special education and in-service training, had hitherto depended upon interschool planning and co-operation.

Responsibilities

The DES pamphlet (1988a) summarized the responsibilities of governors as follows:

Governors
- are responsible for the general conduct of the school
- must have a view on the appropriate curriculum for the school, in the light of the local authority's general policies
- decide whether sex education should be provided at the school
- may offer the headteacher general principles to follow in determining a policy on discipline
- have control over a sum of money handed down to them by the local authority, to cover expenditure on books, equipment and stationery
- may take part in the procedures for selecting the school's staff
- must make information about the school available to parents
- are responsible for preparing an annual report to parents and for holding an annual meeting with the parents to discuss the report and any other matters concerning the running of the school.

At voluntary aided schools, governors have responsibility in addition for:
- controlling the content of the curriculum, and determining the nature of religious instruction
- deciding which children should be admitted to the school

- employing staff
- keeping the building in good repair.

GOVERNORS AND THE EDUCATION REFORM ACT 1988

We now reach the last stage of the story of how the role of governors was dramatically changed between 1975, when the Taylor Committee was set up, and 1988. The government used the new and more powerful school governing body created in 1986 as the legal construct upon which to place considerable responsibility from 1988, for the National Curriculum, the assessment of pupils, the local management of schools, charging for some elements of education, the admission of pupils and, crucially, the decision whether to apply for grant-maintained status. The thrusting of the individual school into salience as the focus of policy delivery was completed.

AREAS OF GOVERNORS' INFLUENCE

We are now in a position, therefore, to be able to list the main features of school life and work over which governors have control or influence. Remember that within these broad principles there will always be room for a particular style and balance to be created at any individual school, depending upon the personalities and attitudes of the governors (especially the chair of the governors) and of the teachers (especially the headteacher). But it is important that, as a teacher, you should know the ground rules which all concerned have to follow.

The conduct of the school

The governors have responsibility for the 'conduct of the school', which is described as being 'under the direction' of the governing body (Section 16(1) of the Education (No. 2) Act 1986). This responsibility covers all those intangible matters of attitude and value which go to make up the lifestyle of a school – its ethos. In fact, of course, many of these are in the hands of the headteacher and other teachers, because they are matters that depend crucially on how the daily tasks are carried out. The headteacher is charged with the 'determination and organisation of the secular curriculum' (Section 18(5)). Thus the legislation creates a requirement for co-operation between the lay governors and the headteacher and staff if a school is to be an effective community. The governors' power ultimately lies in the ability to call for reports and explanations and to make their views on the conduct of the school clear and public. In extreme circumstances they have considerable disciplinary power, but in normal circumstances the expectation would be that governors give support within and beyond the school to the body of teachers whose general lines of work (but not the detail) they have approved.

Curriculum

Section 1(1) of the Education Reform Act 1988 makes it the unequivocal duty of the governing body to ensure that the National Curriculum and the legal requirements for religious education are implemented. However, the responsibility is also given to the local education authority and the headteacher. Again, therefore, the requirement for co-operation is implicit and becomes more clear in the process by which any individual school's curriculum would be determined. The National Curriculum is the national requirement; but each LEA and school has to put its own gloss on it. The LEA has a duty to keep curricular policy under review and to prepare and promulgate its own statement of policy. School governors must consider both the National Curriculum (strictly, this means all the Orders made by the Secretary of State) and the LEA policy statement. They must then prepare their own policy statement for the school. The governors have a general power to 'modify' the LEA policy, but they cannot ignore it or reject it. They must consult the LEA on any matters in their statement which would cut across LEA policy. They must also consult the headteacher and 'have regard' to any representations made by the local community. There is a particular duty to consult the chief officer of police for their area.

The object of all this is to provide that the National Curriculum can be tailored a little to local needs. But the governors must follow the National Curriculum, in the light of the LEA's policy, as modified by the governors. The reality in most schools is that the headteacher and other teachers prepare a curriculum statement for consideration by the governors, and this is usually agreed without major amendment. But the governors have the right – indeed the duty – to consider detail and to ask for a full explanation on any aspect they may wish.

Sex education

The Education (No. 2) Act 1986 gave the governors a special part to play in determining school policy on sex education, and it is restated in the 1988 Act and extended to grant-maintained schools. It is the governors who can decide whether there is to be any sex education in the school or none. If they think there should be some, they must 'make and keep up to date' a written statement on the content and organization of such teaching. The 1988 Act further required that if sex education is to be given, it must be 'in such a manner as to encourage . . . pupils to have due regard to moral considerations and the value of family life' (Section 46). It must be noted, however, that any syllabus required for a public examination could be taught – so that, for example, a ban on sex education by the governors would not inhibit the teaching of biology.

The governors must also have regard to Section 28 of the Local Government Act 1988, which forbids local authorities from any action which would (Maclure, 1992: 149):

a) intentionally promote homosexuality or publish material with the intention of promoting homosexuality.

b) promote the teaching in any maintained school for the acceptability of homosexuality as a pretended family relationship.

Political balance

Governors have a duty (along with LEAs and headteachers) to secure 'a balanced presentation of opposing views' on controversial topics in lessons or school-organized extra-curricular activities (Education (No. 2) Act 1986, Section 45).

Length of the school day

Governors can now fix the times of schools sessions (that is, the school day and how it is divided between morning and afternoon). The LEA continues to determine the school terms within the academic year. LEAs can advise and warn about school days and parents must be given adequate notice of any proposed change. The intention behind putting control over the length of the school day with the governors was to allow extensions to cope with the National Curriculum, where deemed necessary, and experiments such as the 'continental day' (the omission of lunch-time).

Complaints and appeals

The governors have been made the first point of complaint for any parent who is dissatisfied with the work of the school, and in particular with whether the National Curriculum is being provided ('delivered') adequately. Beyond the governors, if they fail to satisfy the parent(s), is an appeals machinery set up by the LEA.

Appointments and dismissals of staff

As was seen in Chapter 3, the governors have wide powers in the appointment and dismissal of teaching and non-teaching staff, derived from their responsibility for the delegated school budget. The chief education officer (CEO) of the LEA has a right to give advice over the appointment of headteachers and deputies, which the governors must consider. The CEO must also give advice on the appointment of other staff, if the governors ask for it. The headteacher has a right to advise on the appointment of all staff other than the headteacher.

The School Teachers' Pay and Conditions Act (1991) further strengthened the position of governors. Teachers' contracts may not in future include any provisions on pay, duties and working time in addition to those specified in a Pay and Conditions Order made under the 1991 Act. That is, the LEA may not import into a teacher's contract such features as a limit on the size of classes to be taught, which would cut across a governing body's responsibility to manage and take its own decisions on priorities. The anomaly, inherent since 1988, arising from the 'double source of employment' (LEAs and governors) in county schools has been emphatically resolved in favour of the governors.

Discipline

The discipline of the school falls within the governors' general responsibilities for the conduct of the school. The governors must prepare 'a written statement of general principles' and the headteacher must act in accordance with it and also 'have regard to any guidance the governors may offer on particular matters'. However, the 1986 Act makes it clear that the headteacher carries the main responsibility for making school rules and seeing they are enforced (Section 22(a)).

The 1986 Act also tried to clarify and strengthen the rules governing the suspension or expulsion of pupils from school. In law, this is now known as 'exclusion', temporary, indefinite or permanent. It is complicated territory and the rules differ a little between county, controlled and aided schools. However, the essence of the 1986 Act was to introduce 'due process' for the protection of all concerned, and especially the pupil. At every stage, parents can make representations and governors must act in accordance with the articles of government and LEA guidance.

If a pupil is permanently excluded, Section 26 of the 1986 Act provides for a formal appeals procedure to be used by the parent or the pupil (if over the age of 18). The decision of the Appeals Committee is binding in the case of county or controlled schools. In an aided or special-agreement school, the governors retain the final right of decision on whether to readmit a pupil.

Finance

The 1988 Act gave governors wide discretion over the spending of the budget provided under the LEA's scheme of delegation. All the pressure from the DES since 1988 has been in the direction of urging LEAs to delegate a wider responsibility for finances to governors. There is a last-resort power left with LEAs, which can withdraw a governing body's delegated powers if governors are guilty of 'substantial and persistent failure' to comply with the scheme, or where their stewardship is not being discharged 'in a satisfactory manner'. There has not yet (1992) been any instance of any LEA using this power, and the legal tussle that might be entailed in its use can so far be only imagined.

Charges

Sections 106–111 of the 1988 Act gave governors unprecedented power to levy charges on parents for activities connected with the school. There cannot be any charge for admission or in-school curricular tuition: but that leaves a range of normal school activities for which a charge can be made.

School governors: landmarks

1944   Education Act – requires the appointment of governors (secondary) and managers (primary)

1976   Auld Report – William Tyndale School

1977   Taylor Report – recommends wider powers and constitution

1978   *The Composition of Governing Bodies* – White Paper and Education Bill (fell 1979)

1980   Education Act – new powers and constitution for governing bodies (some clauses not operative until 1985)

1984   *Parental Influence at School: A New Framework for School Government* – DES discussion paper

1985   *Better Schools* – White Paper

1986   Education (No. 2) Act – radical reform of powers and constitution of governing bodies; present framework put in place.

1988   Education Reform Act – extended powers of governors

1991   School Teachers' Pay and Conditions Act – further strengthened powers of governors

1992   Education (Schools) Act

Grant-maintained status

It is the governors of a maintained or voluntary school who, under conditions laid down by the 1988 Act, have the right to seek grant-maintained status from the Secretary of State – that is, to 'opt out' of LEA control.

Reports and meetings

The governors must prepare an annual report, to be sent to every parent, containing the name and status of each governor, as well as a financial report, the examination and assessment results, and steps taken to strengthen links with the community.

CONCLUSION

The governing bodies of schools emerged from the 1986 and 1988 Acts not only with considerable additional powers but also with considerably greater expectations laid upon them. They will not be left unscrutinized in the discharge of these new and extended responsibilities. The intention of the 1988 Act is that parents will be able to hold the school (that is, the governors) accountable to a far greater extent because of the additional information they will regularly be given. The 1992 Education (Schools) Act reinforced this. The LEA will also be expected to monitor the performance of governing bodies and, especially, hold them accountable for the use of delegated funds. The outcome of this new balance of power and responsibility will become apparent during the 1990s.

PART 3

TRYING TO MAKE SENSE OF IT

Introduction to Part 3

If you have read all or most of this book so far, you will have gained a good deal of knowledge about what has changed in the past thirty years in the control of education. The two most striking facts are that so many more aspects and processes *are* controlled now, compared with a *laissez-faire* approach earlier; and that the locus of control is almost entirely now with central government, compared with a deliberate dispersal of power formerly. There has been a dramatic increase in both the *amount* of control and its *concentration* at the centre. It must also be said that there has been a determination in government to *use* its powers. The Secretary of State's intervention in the summer of 1992 into the workings of the GCSE examination concerning comparability of grades between examining boards illustrates the point. Furthermore, the Minister of State told the Examination Boards Conference in September 1992 that 'Ministers are taking direct responsibility for examinations at age 16 under the national curriculum' and made it clear that ministers intended 'not only to pursue a more hands on approach to the examinations but also to the content of the syllabus' (*The Independent*, 25 September 1992). The period since 1988 is full of such direct and piecemeal interventions, ranging over assessment procedures, the primary curriculum, special educational needs, school funding and virtually every other aspect of school policy.

Before reading further in this final part, go back for a moment to the Preface, where I compared the world as John Vaizey analysed it in 1963 with my account thirty years on. He described a public service in which the main levers of power were through finance. Finance remains, of course, the single most significant method and source of control; but to it has been added direct control of many other dimensions which Vaizey did not mention, and he could be understood by his audience when he tacitly implied that they were controlled either through the consensual value system or through the workings of *laissez-faire* within a pluralist system. They now include school curriculum and examinations; the assessment of pupils and appraisal of teachers; the curriculum and structures of teacher training; the format for the regular inspection of schools; and the detailed formulae for individual school budgets and the funding of sixth-form and further-education colleges.

This, in short, is *what* happened. The question is, *why* did it happen? Often, as a particular part of the story was being told, a kind of explanatory strand seemed to appear. Do these explanatory strands form a fabric? And if they do, who were the weavers, who the designers of the pattern? The search for cause, even meaning, in history is a moral responsibility of the historian. But in dealing with any age, humility is required, and never more than when analysing recent events, in many of which the writer has also been actor. I shall, therefore, try to use perspectives drawn from politics and sociology as well as history, and introduce several analytical frameworks. The result will be less tidy and the picture probably less comprehensible, but the reader will have more freedom to take the argument forward personally and to recall and press into use these tools of analysis for other purposes also. I then offer some thoughts of my own towards an explanation, which do not belong in any single theoretical standpoint, but arise from a historical perspective rooted in the spirit of toleration and sceptical humanism which goes back to More and Montaigne, and before them to the classical world. In that historical cast of mind, I reflect on both my own experience of action in the past thirty years and the longer record recounted in this book.

The whole is not intended, however, as a weighty treatise, rather as some speculations and starting points for understanding the extraordinary changes in education that have come about in the past twenty years and within which you, as a student and then a 'starting teacher', will find yourself operating.

One essential part of the story, namely the work and fate of the LEAs, has not yet been told. To a large extent, an analysis of that story points to explanations for change throughout the system. So we will start by looking at the changing functions of the local education authorities. The last chapter will move from there into a broader analysis of central government policies.

CHAPTER 9

The local education authorities 1965–92

One approach to the question 'Why did it happen?' is to look at the fate of the LEAs. The single most dramatic structural and political change between 1972 and 1992 is the reduction of the LEA. For the whole century, since their creation in 1902, LEAs had been at the hub of both administration and development. They were seen as having many practical and constitutional advantages. They were locally accountable as part of elected local government, and a useful means by which general policy could be adapted to local conditions and aspirations. They thus encouraged throughout the country democratic ways of thinking and working. They avoided the necessity to centralize power and the tiresome detail that would fall upon civil servants if it were centralized. They could be both agents of central policy (capital building programmes, the teachers quota – which attempted to ration teacher supply fairly among different areas of the country, 'Hadow' reorganization of all-age schools, etc.) and at the same time the wellspring of local innovation. The memoirs of a distinguished chief education officer opened with a chapter called 'L.E.A. = leader' (Wilson, 1985), and I have drawn attention elsewhere to the proud record of innovation in LEAs (Tomlinson, 1986b: 220):

> The record shows that not only the variety of education but also its quality has been improved through the work of LEAs and their schools. By supporting innovation, encouraging good practice, giving freedom of action to imaginative professionals, the LEAs have been the seed-bed for significant educational advances, including many now being generalised by central government

policy. I have always regretted how much this developmental role has been ignored or understated in the literature; perhaps that has contributed to the present pathology. The sensitive LEA has very many ways in which to influence and encourage strivings towards improvement. By the way it designs, furnishes and equips buildings it creates the basis of the environment for learning; by the appointment of teachers and support staff and their in-service training it contributes to the capacity and morale of teachers and their collaborators. Its staffing policies, the spirit and extent of its consultative procedures, the flexibility of its financial and administrative arrangements, the appointment and support of advisers and inspectors, relationships with other professional services and with community groups, and the contributions its members and officers make to national educational development – in all these and many other ways LEAs have created and still create not merely diversity but quality and progress. Consider any catalogue of significant educational developments in this country this century and I suspect you will find LEA involvement – often an LEA initiative – even though for much of that time broad curriculum policies were centrally directed or were much influenced by public examinations subject to central direction. Let me offer a few – self-evaluation by schools, middle schools, the open primary school, school curriculum statements, training in management for headteachers, schools as cost centres, school-based curriculum development, profiling and records of achievement, curriculum-based staffing, residential curriculum centres, teachers' centres, the school psychological services, graded tests, education and industry liaison, community out-reach in early childhood education, outdoor education centres.

LEAs appeared to be the essential engine of the national/local education system. Yet it took less than ten years to reduce them to the residual status proposed by the White Paper of 1992, *Choice and Diversity* (DFE, 1992a), and the subsequent Education Bill.

Two sets of forces achieved this. One was the positive determination of the new right governments of the 1980s to pursue certain goals; the other was the weaknesses or failings of some LEAs, combined with the fact that local government has no independent constitutional status in Britain (as it has in some countries), but is simply a creature of central government. Here is a crude summary of examples of both these forces at work.

GOVERNMENT POLICIES TOWARDS LOCAL GOVERNMENT

New right Conservatism proposed the removal or reduction as far as possible of all institutions intermediate between the state and the individual; hence, for example, the attack on trade unions, professional organizations and local government. In education, teachers' trade unions also claimed to be professional organizations (in the absence of a general teaching council), and thus their reduction to inanition between 1984 and 1987 served at least two ends simultaneously. This also paved the way to the Teachers' Pay and Conditions Act 1987 and central control of salaries and conditions of service, an event occasioned at least partly by the failure of LEA and teacher negotiators.

It was also the case that since LEAs were part of local government they were bound to suffer from the general determination to reduce its powers. The need for financial retrenchment from the mid-1970s reinforced this, since education represented about 60 per cent of local government expenditure at the top tier. The financial screw was turned yet tighter once school rolls began to fall and school places had to be taken out of use. This in turn led to acrimonious exchanges between central and local government when on occasions a Secretary of State would refuse, apparently on party political grounds, to close a school as proposed by an LEA. In short, a period of financial constraint, absolute contraction and ideological distaste created a totally different frame of relationships between central and local government, and perhaps pre-eminently so – more than in any other local government service – in education, which had relied so much upon open relationships. Ideas of partnership, consensus and common cause died on the spikes of Department of the Environment decisions about the rate support grant or staffing-level controls or 'cash limits', of Audit Commission reports on surplus school places or further education, or of general requirements for competitive tendering, as much as on directions from the DES about curriculum or capital building programmes or school governing bodies. In the end, the fact that the local administration of the education service had been embedded within local government as a whole, seen as an advantage for so long, not only gave no strength or protection when the tide turned; it actually caused the water to rise faster. And this was not only because of the animus and determination of central government: weaknesses within local government itself also contributed.

ATTITUDES TO EDUCATION WITHIN LOCAL GOVERNMENT

The ideal of 'corporatism'

From at least the late 1960s, local government, from within and without, was urged to think and act more 'corporately'; that is, to look at its range of services not separately but as interacting, interdependent and forming a whole when received by the citizen. 'The local authority itself, and not its committees, is responsible for the provision of services. Departmentalism . . . hampers authorities from assessing the problems of their areas comprehensively and deciding priorities within each service but also between services' (Interim Report to the Study Group on Local Authority Management Structures, para. 13, quoted DOE, 1972: para. 13, p. 132). It was, and remains, a beguiling ideal. From the point of view of education, however, there were at least two problems with this philosophy. As the largest service, it could be all too easily seen as the one that must most 'adjust' in any corporate plans – which in effect meant yielding ground or finance or both. The conspicuous success of so many LEAs in developing community schools, which included other local services in an integrated whole, ironically only made the matter worse in the eyes of those outside education who wanted part of the new action of corporatism. Pioneers are seldom liked by the later settlers.

This problem was sharply analysed by Derek Senior in his one-man minority report to the Local Government Royal Commission of 1968. He called education 'The cuckoo in the nest' (HMSO, 1969). The implication was twofold: cuckoos were typically greedy and ate food intended for others; and they were aliens in the first place. This second point, that despite half a century's history it could be argued that education did not really fit into local government, was also one that had refused to go away over the years and which Senior himself emphasized. It had been held since 1902 and before that education ought to be seen as 'a seamless robe' – that is, that all the elements of the service outside the autonomous universities needed to be within the purview and responsibility of a single authority if they were to be planned and delivered most effectively. It had led to a continual argument about the size of LEA required for effectiveness. 'The most obstinate of the problems of educational administration is how to combine local knowledge, initiative and accessibility with an area large enough to provide

149

a satisfactory unit.' Lady Simon, a member of the Manchester Education Committee, wrote that in 1949; and she called her address on that occasion to the annual conference of Divisional Executives 'The present education muddle and the way out' (quoted Fiske, 1975: 1). Derek Senior, twenty years later, argued that since 1944, education had been in reality a national service with nationally determined policies and nationally determined standards. As a result, education (the education committee, the chief education officer and his or her staff) held a 'half-alien' position within the local authority. Senior concluded that if local government were to be reformed on principles that suited the education service, we should finish by creating a structure 'seriously and increasingly ill-adapted to all the main functions that lie at the heart of local democracy' (HMSO, 1969: Vol. II, para. 323, p. 75).

In the event, neither Derek Senior's nor Redcliffe-Maud's proposals for local government reform were fully enshrined in the Local Government Act of 1972, a political compromise which came into effect in 1974. LEAs of varying sizes, from 100,000 to 1.3 million, were created. Crucially, the legal requirements to appoint an education committee and a chief education officer were retained. However, 'corporatism' remained a salient objective, especially among the new breed of chief executives whose role largely depended upon its development. During the first half of the 1970s, the most visible national indication of local government's determination to rein in the education service was the campaign between 1972 and 1977 to get rid of 'the single national organisation and voice for education'; that is to say, the Association of Education Committees (AEC). The AEC had been created in 1902 at the same time as LEAs to bridge the gap between the two kinds of LEA, the county and the town. Neither the Association of County Councils (ACC – CCA before 1974) nor the Association of Metropolitan Authorities (AMA – AMC before 1974) could claim to speak to government or teachers or public for all LEAs; the Association of Education Committees both could and did. It was upon its recommendation, for example, that the Burnham Committee was first set up; and especially from 1945 to 1970 it had been very influential in all central policy formation. This, of course, only served to emphasize the 'alien' nature of education within local government. From 1972, the newly formed associations representing county councils and municipal authorities determined upon the demise of the AEC. Despite the wish of many members of education committees from all the major political parties to retain the AEC, they found themselves under increasing 'pressure to conform to the negative official line of the AMA and ACC' (Cooke and Gosden, 1986: 95).

At first the stance taken by the DES was phlegmatic. In July 1973, the Permanent Secretary (William Pile) wrote to the Secretary of the AEC assuring him that there would be 'no diminution in the Department's support (witness the Whitehall scars we bear) for the continued existence of strong and influential education committees throughout the country' (quoted Cooke and Gosden, 1986: 92). Only a year later, however, Reg Prentice, the new Labour Secretary of State, wrote to inform the AEC that he had decided to remove it from the Burnham Committee from September 1974. Since the AEC had provided both the secretariat and the accommodation for Burnham, the symbolic effect, as intended, was mortal. Although about one-third of LEAs remained in membership until the end, it became clear that the AEC had been squeezed out, and in 1977 it was wound up.

The campaign against the special status of education committees – *imperium in imperio*, an empire within an empire – led to a feeling among many education officers that the values of the service must be set higher than those of staying within local government, desirable though that remained for general democratic reasons. In 1973, in one of its first public statements, the newly formed Society of Education Officers (SEO) which had been created by amalgamating the former separate Associations of Chief Education Officers and of Education Officers, argued forcibly for the principles of partnership and proclaimed themselves 'all local government men'. But at the same time they set out in principles – nineteen in all – the conditions which would have to be satisfied if education were to be able to remain effective as a service within local government, and made it clear that they were not 'local government men at any price' (SEO, 1973). This is a chilling statement, viewed twenty years on. On the one hand, the rest of local government took no notice, even though 60 per cent of their status and finance was at stake; on the other, the education officers made the assumption that their role would continue come what may – that only its location was in contention. This can be seen now as a double act of hubris. Local government is indeed now diminished, not least by the effective loss of education; and the role of LEA/education officer has largely been dispersed, dissolved and redistributed between the centre, the funding councils and the schools and colleges.

OTHER ISSUES

In addition to the factors already identified, of central government's antipathy to local government after 1979 and local government's carelessness with its education service, there are several small but important issues which promoted the demise of the LEA, and one overriding force, namely finance. Among the significant irritants was the left-wing political extremism of some LEAs, which served to feed the new right determination to extirpate socialism. Education was particularly vulnerable to accusations, whether ill-founded or not, that corporate policies on race, sexual equality or disability were being forced into schools and distorting the curriculum and methods of teaching. This was chiefly though not entirely a phenomenon of the London boroughs and ILEA, and they were cheek-by-jowl with Westminster. Government attitudes were hardened by the fact that in the financial sense ILEA was unaccountable to central government, because as a result of the government formulae of the 1980s it received no central government grants. Having abolished the Greater London Council in 1985, the government abolished ILEA in a last-minute clause of the 1988 Education Reform Act.

The way in which controls over local government finance were used by central government both to reduce the amount of discretion available to LEAs and at the same time to convert them to an agency of Whitehall is an essential part of the story of how LEAs were diminished. The Labour government of the late 1970s introduced 'cash limits' on the central government rate support grant, which meant that if services were to be maintained in periods of inflation the difference had to be met from local taxation – at that time, the rates. The Conservative governments carried the process further and faster. New 'block grant' arrangements from 1981–2 were based on government assessments of what a local authority ought to spend (grant-related expenditure), and then contained built-in penalties if targets were overspent. By 1984, rate-capping legislation had been introduced, which in effect controlled the amount that could be raised from local taxation, whatever the views of the local electorate might be. If local authorities spent above government target they lost grant, and the difference could not be made up from the rates. Local government expenditure had been closed at both ends. Allied to this reduction in local discretion, central 'ear-marked' grants were increasingly introduced to finance policies directed by central government.

Education Support Grants (ESGs), proposed in 1983 and introduced progressively from 1985–6, were the vehicle for this policy in education. The details of financial policy towards local government in the 1980s are complex, but the essentials are clear: 'the LEAs were tied down and cut back' (Cooke and Gosden, 1986: 132). This prepared the way for the massive advent of central control of educational policies from 1986.

1992

And thus we arrive at the position in 1992, when the much-heralded White Paper, which is to set the administrative framework for education for a quarter of a century, devotes only seven paragraphs to the functions of the LEA. The picture is one that had been predicted by some during the run-up to the 1988 Act (see, for example, Campbell *et al.*, 1987), of the LEA as authority of the last resort, being left to cope with those pupils rejected by the market in schools, and providing services such as special education and transport which represent market failures. The Education Bill of 1992 even proposed the removal of the statutory requirement to appoint an education committee, so that what functions do remain to an LEA may well be overseen by a variety of committees, none with education as its main concern.

The immediate background is that the LEA, once the authority responsible for the 'seamless robe' of all education outside the universities from the cradle to the grave, had already had taken away from it higher education (1988) and further education and sixth-form colleges (1992). It had become therefore a 'schools authority', with some residual and exiguous powers to provide adult education. Some saw this as paving the way to giving the LEA responsibility to the district councils in counties and to resurgent cities, such as Southampton and Leicester, which had become districts in 1974 but might regain their 'independent' status. In fact, a totally different approach was adopted. Since the government's prime objective was to persuade as many schools as possible to vote for grant-maintained status, a national schools funding agency was proposed. It was both to act as a buffer between the Department for Education (DFE) and schools already grant maintained, and to have concurrent duties with the LEA for planning school places in the interim. 'When 75% of the Secondary (or primary) pupils in the LEA are in Grant Maintained schools . . . the Funding Agency will discharge the duty by itself' (DFE,

1992a: 19). Moreover, 'the LEA may apply to be relieved of this responsibility well before that point is reached'.

This is the solution proposed to the problem identified by commentators since 1987, that there are some necessary functions which schools acting autonomously cannot perform for themselves. The government, in the White Paper of 1992, describes these functions as follows (DFE, 1992a: 19–20):

> 3.5 There are, however, some functions that even autonomous schools cannot carry out for themselves. For example, someone has to calculate levels of current and capital funding and pay relevant grants to schools. Schools' use of public funds needs to be subject to scrutiny and audit. These tasks currently fall to the Department for Education. As the number of GM [grant-maintained] schools grows, it will become increasingly inefficient and inappropriate for these essentially executive tasks to be performed by a Department of State.
>
> 3.6 Furthermore it will also become increasingly difficult for the LEA on its own to secure, as is its duty, that there are sufficient, suitable primary and secondary school places available in the area, and to ensure that every child of compulsory school age is being suitably educated. Nor can these responsibilities fall to individual GM schools even though they will have an increasing part to play, as the number of places they provide grows: there is a need for a new body which can share this duty and which is separate from and can make proposals to the Secretary of State.

It is these functions, now admitted to exist by a government that hitherto had appeared to maintain that a market place of 25,000 autonomous, competing schools would create the millennium, that will be given to the Funding Agency once 75 per cent of either primary or secondary schools are grant maintained, or earlier if the LEA so requests. Any basis in democratically elected local government has been removed.

There is a chilling symmetry in all this which suggests that the British are not finding new solutions to their problems of educational administration but merely recycling old ones. The LEA was invented by the 1902 Education Act and survived, just, until the Education Act of 1992 and the White Paper of that year. The Bryce Report of 1895 had said, 'On no one point were our witnesses more entirely unanimous than on this – the necessity of local authorities to a national system of Secondary Education' (Maclure, 1968: 143). It continued, however, to say that there was no agreement about how such local authorities should be constituted, the size of their domains, or their powers *vis-à-vis* the schools. The alternative to the local authority system, which Bryce firmly rejected, would be a centralized control of schools. The seeds of 1992 are clear to see.

We do not yet know what the legislation following the White Paper will contain nor what will ensue from the new law. A perspicacious chief education officer has, however, risked a guess. Anne Sofer of Tower Hamlets suggests that there will be three different kinds of reaction from LEAs. The Ostrich Tendency will believe that opting out will not become widespread and little significant change will therefore occur. The Pragmatic Collaborators will promise to do everything possible to make the new arrangements work well, and ensure that thus 'the partnership between national and local government is sustained'. (In fact, they will eventually kill off any partnership.) The Mavericks will urge that LEAs should 'accept the fact that the Government has written local accountability out of the picture . . . and therefore believe that the sooner functions are transferred in an orderly fashion to the Funding Agency the better' (Sofer, 1992: 13).

Meanwhile, LEAs seem to be moving inexorably towards a role as provider of a limited range of 'pupil-specific services' which schools cannot or do not wish to provide, and also to becoming, as some had predicted, 'the authority of last resort' for pupils excluded from 'autonomous' schools. What forms of new provision may be developed in consequence is as yet unclear.

This state of confusion and uncertainty arises at least in part from rapid changes of emphasis in policy. Kenneth Baker thought that the two really important aspects of 'his' 1988 Education Reform Act were the National Curriculum and the local financial management of schools. He did not rate the idea of grant-maintained status for schools very highly. Kenneth Clarke, by contrast, pushed the idea of grant-maintained status hard, and therefore created the necessity for a system to replace the LEA. It was this problem that the White Paper of 1992 started to address, however incompletely. We are thus in a very different context of education legislation in the 1990s from that of the 1940s or even the 1970s. Whereas in the past legislation provided for a system and then for delegation of some powers to schools, now we start with the autonomous school and wait to see what else may be needed.

When it is put to government that such a process will unavoidably give rise to, for example, inequities in arrangements for admissions to schools, or difficulties in providing for pupils with special needs, and, above all, the general loss of any common value system, the rejoinder is that the values of the market in providing for consumer choice are to be deemed of more importance. The implication is that those other values

155

The local education authorities: landmarks

1902   LEAs created

1944   Education Act – LEAs made the providers of education service under general direction of Board of Education

1969   Redcliffe-Maud Report – Royal Commission on reform of local government; minority report by Derek Senior describes education as 'the cuckoo in the nest'

1971   Bains Report – corporatism in local government advocated

1974   Reform of local government – many new LEAs

1977   Closure of Association of Education Committees (begun 1903)

1981   Government block grant based on 'grant-related expenditure'

1984   Rate-capping; Education Support Grants (central government direction of LEAs)

1988   Inner London Education Authority (ILEA) abolished

1988   Education Act – encourages market in schools and introduces new forms of non-LEA school and local financial management for all schools; removes higher education from LEAs

1989   Audit Commission Report on future for LEAs, *Losing an Empire and Finding a Role*

1992   Education (Schools) Act; Education (Further and Higher Education) Act

1993   Education Bill proposes removal of statutory requirement for an education committee in LEAs and only residual powers/duties for LEAs

---

belong in an earlier and now abandoned set of beliefs connected with promoting equity, equality and social justice. The true neo-liberal would echo Friedrich von Hayek, the doyen of the new economic and social liberalism, who observed that social justice, as a concept, is 'entirely empty and meaningless'.

The demise of the LEAs was caused, therefore, by the confluence of many forces. The internal doubts and jealousies of the rest of local government played their part; so did the hubris of some in education. The political extremism of some LEAs played a part; so did the failure of some LEAs to innovate. But the predominant reason for the dramatic reduction of the

LEAs in the 1980s and early 1990s lay in a powerful combination of political ideology with political detestation of the LEA in particular. Other aspects of local government actually had their powers and duties increased or added to in this period. Moreover, models for a sensible role for the LEA were on offer, in, for example, the recommendations of the Audit Commission (1989), or in the health services, where district health authorities were converted into purchasers of services and guardians of quality. Departments of social work service moved in the same direction through the Children Act 1989. The inescapable conclusion is that the LEAs attracted an irrational degree of dislike from government, and thus educational government in the 1990s, locally and centrally, will be faced with the consequences of the vacuum that has been created.

One thing is clear: new teachers will not necessarily be able to rely on the structures and support formerly provided by most LEAs: the new teacher's world has been collapsed, for good or ill, to the microcosm – some might say the parish pump – of the school.

CHAPTER 10

Central government policies for education since 1979

We have seen how it happened that by the time the first Thatcher government was elected in 1979, the so-called political consensus of the post-war years had given way to concern about standards in the teaching of basic subjects, about some manifestations of new teaching methods (the William Tyndale case: ILEA, 1976), and about the narrowness of the primary curriculum and the over-elaboration of that after age 14 (HMI surveys), and to controversy about forms of secondary-school organization. At a deeper level, there was concern about both the efficacy of education as a major contributor to social improvement and its failure to contribute to economic effectiveness. We have also seen that at first the Conservative government carried over, to a large extent, the agenda announced in James Callaghan's Ruskin Speech of 1976, albeit through very different methods. Then, in the third Thatcher administration from 1987, a radical phase asserted itself, creating the structures and climate of the time of writing (1992).

THE INTRINSIC/EXTRINSIC ARGUMENT ABOUT EDUCATION

It will be helpful to dispose of (or, at least, to expose) one enduring argument about the nature and purposes of education before analysing the particular party political standpoints of the

1980s. It will help explain how the governments of that decade in one sense behaved no differently from governments of other periods, although the emphases and techniques were particular. The argument is the intrinsic/extrinsic one:

- *Education as 'extrinsic'*. From this standpoint, the education of the individual is primarily to serve the purposes of society, the economy, or other organization providing it (churches, or sectarian or civil groups). Education is provided primarily as an induction into the culture so that the individual may serve the purposes of that society or group as effectively as possible.
- *Education as 'intrinsic'*. From this standpoint, education is justified by the way in which it confers freedom upon those who receive it. Its prime object is the creation of an autonomous, critical, free frame of mind (in both teacher and taught). The individual is then free to contribute creatively to the development of the culture.

This debate is both very old (it goes back in the written record at least to Plato and Confucius) and also, for all practical purposes, unnecessary.

A curriculum to be justifiable needs to contain at least three elements:

1 the 'transmission of knowledge';
2 the development of the individual's mental powers and personal capacities;
3 an introduction into the mores of the civil society concerned.

As we have seen, in our examination of curriculum, the questions arise about which knowledge and who decides, which social mores should be salient, and what should be the balance between direct transmission of knowledge and the development of individual critical capacity. The Conservative governments' actions 1979–92 give an almost text-book series of examples of the pitfalls of blundering unprepared, or prepared with partial and prejudiced notions, into this complex field. Hence the continuing readjustments of the National Curriculum and assessment since 1988.

THE IDEAS OF THE NEW RIGHT

It is important to understand that the ideas of the new right which became so influential as the basis of an aggressive Conservatism in the 1980s were a long time in the making. For example, Von Hayek's *The Road to Serfdom*, an early bugle-call of new right ideas, was published in the same year as the 1944 Education Act was put on the statute book. The maturation process continued during and fed upon the long period of post-war consensus. That, together with the appeal of the new right's ideas to an even older tradition – the free-market principles of the eighteenth and nineteenth centuries – helps to account for their potency, once they found a congenial political climate.

The corpus of new right ideas about education consisted of a mixture of general political objectives, most of which would bear on a public education service, and specific notions about the purposes of education and how it should be structured. At the risk of oversimplification, it may be helpful to list some members of the two categories by way of illustration.

General

The resurgence of Conservative and anti-socialist thought which has occurred in the UK, the USA, France and elsewhere since the 1970s contains four fundamental elements:

1   a belief that the market will distribute scarce resources more effectively than any other method, such as planning, whether by the state or groups within the state;
2   a belief in the individual as the relevant unit of action. Everything possible should therefore be done to remove regulations and structures that fetter freedom of individual action. There is an attachment to individual choice rather than acceptance of historical necessity;
3   linked chiefly with (2) above, a belief that socialism in its concern for the corporate and interdependent aspects of life had weakened the position and motivation of the individual. The extirpation of socialism therefore becomes an aim;
4   also connected with (2) above, but structural rather than political, a belief that so far as possible all organizations and structures intermediate between the individual and the sovereign state should be removed or reduced considerably in power and influence.

It follows from these principles that the public sector ought to be diminished as a proportion of national economic activity, and the private sector – based on the free enterprise of individuals – encouraged. It also follows that 'the consumer' should be regarded as more important than 'the producer', especially in any process where there is an element of monopoly, whether through a public service or otherwise. Likewise, following from (4) above, trade unions, professional organizations and local government need to be reduced in influence, if not removed.

The first two Thatcher administrations, 1979–87, applied this philosophy energetically. Public expenditure was reined in and a process of 'privatization' of public services begun. The trade unions were given little or no part in government planning, and the National Union of Mineworkers (the flagship of 'old unionism') was reduced after a prolonged and bitter strike. Although opinion remains divided about the extent of the 'Thatcher Revolution' (Kavanagh and Seldon, 1989), there is little doubt that a distinctive style and requirement for conformity of thought among those working in or with government became the hallmark of the period and constituted a radical new value system.

Education

Let us now look at the new right's aims for education. The main objectives may be summarized as:

1 higher standards;
2 value for money;
3 accountability.

The sub-objectives were to:

1 reduce 'producer domination';
2 reduce the influence of local government (including LEAs);
3 reduce public expenditure as a proportion of gross national product;
4 expunge 'progressive' elements;
5 increase vocational elements in the curriculum.

We have seen that the methods used to pursue these broad and often fuzzy objectives were through central controls, and the market.

We shall examine in a minute why two apparently contradictory methodologies could be pressed into use simultaneously and by the same administration. Let us recall first what had been done between 1979 and 1992 in consequence:

control:

- teacher training: curriculum and structures (from 1983);
- National Curriculum;
- assessment if pupils at 7, 11, 14 and 16;
- school external examinations;
- teacher appraisal;
- school inspections every four years;
- formulae for school budgets;
- earmarked central funding rather than general grant (e.g. INSET);
- removal of higher and further education from LEAs;
- control of LEA expenditure on schools by rate-capping or charge-capping and central grants based on spending targets, etc.;
- proposal for a schools funding agency;
- transfer of most LEA powers to central government or governing bodies or proposed schools funding agency.

market:

- open enrolment (competition);
- variety of schools (maintained, grant-maintained, city technology college, assisted places);
- devolution of powers to governing bodies;
- local management of schools;
- complaints procedures;
- information to parents;
- school inspection reports.

FACTIONS AND POWER STRUGGLES WITHIN THE CONSERVATIVE PARTY

Although Margaret Thatcher's dominance of style and philosophy gave an impression of monolithic certainty, in fact the Conservative governments of the 1980s were variously representative of the factions within the party, just as any government is. A simple dichotomy would be between the 'old conservatives' and the 'new radicals'. The first group could

accept centralization for the purposes of efficiency, accountability and the removal of power from socialist local governments. The radicals had their eyes set on the market, parental
freedom of choice, the crushing of producer domination, and
central control over only the basic subjects of the curriculum
(the rest to be determined by the market).

Yet even this broad and crude distinction between 'cen-
tralists' and 'modernizers' will not entirely do. The mind-set
and actions of Sir Keith Joseph, who held the position of
Secretary of State for longer than anyone else between 1979 and
1992, will serve to illustrate the subtleties. Sir Keith Joseph was
a leading intellectual within Conservative circles as the Conservatives' policies took shape in the 1970s. He virtually founded
the Centre for Policy Studies. He was absolutely devoted to the
market in economic affairs and wished to see the principles
extended to the 'social market'. He spoke feelingly along these
lines, just after taking up office, at the Society of Education
Officers' (SEO) annual conference in January 1982. Earlier he
had written: 'The blind, unplanned, uncoordinated wisdom of
the market . . . is overwhelmingly superior to the well-
researched, rational, systematic, well-meaning, co-operative,
science-based, forward looking, statistically respectable plans
of Government (Joseph, 1976).

During his time at the DES (1982–6), there was a practical and
ideological struggle between this utterly *laissez-faire* philosophy and the DES officials who, since their castigation in the
OECD Report of 1975, especially for lack of forward planning,
were determined to gain more control and credibility, and urged
upon ministers the need for financial retrenchment, the closure
of surplus school places and the stiffening of LEAs over their
duties with regard to curriculum, all of which necessitated the
gathering and exercise of power at the centre. The conflict
was never resolved. On the one hand, the official rhetoric,
presumably mainly in the control of officials, did change.
Compare, for example, the opening chapters of the DES's *Brief
Guide* to the education service of 1981 and 1984:

- 1981: opens with a chapter entitled 'A national service
  locally administered', and starts, 'The tradition of decen-
  tralised education in Britain is strong.'
- 1984: the heading and the opening sentence have been
  deleted. The pamphlet now opens: 'The Department of
  Education and Science is responsible for all aspects of
  education in England.'

There could be no more incisive or dramatic illustration of official feeling and determination at the DES. And we have seen how centralism marched forward on many fronts during this time.

Yet, as we have also seen, at the political level Sir Keith Joseph, backed by some of the longer-serving senior officials, kept the notion of partnership with teachers and LEAs alive, while inviting them to engage with the DES and accept a sharper and more accountable definition of their responsibilities. 'The Government has reviewed, *together with its partners*, its policies for school education' (DES, 1985e: para. 2, my emphasis). And when, in the next phase of government, a national curriculum was proposed, Sir Keith Joseph opposed it, and spoke against it in the House of Lords. In this respect, he was remaining true to his colours as a free-marketeer and anti-centralist. But by 1987, there were sufficient in the Conservative Party in the Commons who wanted centralized power to carry the day; and many of them were 'new conservatives' rather than 'old conservatives'. The radical right held up, therefore, at least two faces towards education. (For those who want to take the background to this story to greater depth, Christopher Knight (1990) has analysed *The Making of Tory Education Policy in Post-war Britain 1950–86*. Sadly, it does not deal with the most radical phase since 1986.)

SOME THEORETICAL PERSPECTIVES

Are there theoretical perspectives that will help to deepen our understanding? We have already come across the notion of neo-Conservatism, the new radical right with its roots in the *laissez-faire* economic theories of the eighteenth and nineteenth centuries and its faith in the market. The new right could also be characterized as anti-collectivists. Alongside them, and mainly occupying middle political ground on the left of the Conservative Party, in the Liberal/Democratic parties and the right of the Labour Party are those who could be characterized as pluralists or 'reluctant collectivists'. They do not have blind faith in *laissez-faire* and the market, but believe that the capitalist system is the best currently on offer and needs a mixture of free enterprise and control to ensure both wealth and a measure of equity. This was a long-held and respectable position, not a 1970s compromise. Sir William Beveridge (the wartime architect of the welfare state) believed that freedom was an essential value in itself, but compatible with planning. Real freedom means relief both from the evils of poverty, ignorance and illness *and* from overbearing government.

Beyond these political positions would lie those of radical socialists and Marxists. Marxism had many views of education, and oversimplification would be a travesty. Essentially, however, the position is that since those with power use it to maintain the current distribution of control over the means of production, education is inevitably used more to bolster the status quo than as an instrument of liberation.

A set of theoretical perspectives on education policy-making as a whole has been developed by the course team of the Open University for course E333, Policy-Making in Education. In 'Perspectives on policy-making', Roger Dale, following Grant Harman, Maurice Kogan and others, both describes the methodology of the study of education policy-making and suggests four categories of theoretical approaches, namely: systems theory, pluralism, Marxism, and neo-liberalism (Dale, 1986). These theories constitute different ways in which attempts have been made systematically to interrogate and understand social processes. As you will see, although they are different enough to be distinguishable, they have elements in common. Moreover, they are all more or less rooted in one or more of the academic disciplines of sociology, political science, economics or history. Dale also suggests that those studying education policy-making have used a wide range of theoretical approaches. So remember that any categorization will be incomplete in some sense. Dale lists sixteen 'theoretical positions' related to recent literature (1986: 70). But he goes on to suggest the four broad categories mentioned earlier, which I think will be useful to those setting out on the study of education policy-making for the first time.

Systems theory

The branch of this theory most used in education policy analysis is attributable to David Easton, and assumes that in political life 'all social systems are composed of the interactions among persons: such interactions form the basic units of these systems' (quoted Dale, 1986: 71). In such an analysis, stress is placed on the 'gatekeepers' who control resources and influence policy, such as interest groups, political parties and administrators. Where regulation fails, negative feedback may allow equilibrium to be restored or lead to a new equilibrium.

This theory has value in giving insights into a political system such as Britain's, where predominant characteristics have been continuity and stability. It also relates to notions in political theory about the 'general interest' or the 'public interest' and the way in which an appeal to the 'common good' can be a means of regulating political conflicts. In effect, systems theory is a model of the flow of demand and supply of political satisfaction in a society. What it does not show is what demands may never surface or be allowed to surface, from disadvantaged groups. It also fails to give sufficient credence to the force of ideological and technical factors in determining which 'demands' are allowed and which excluded by those in power. Dale concludes, 'It provides a good picture of how existing holders of political power may defend their position, but does not explain the distribution of power *per se* or its consequences' (1986: 75). My own view is that the radicalization of British politics in the 1980s had made systems theory the least helpful as an interpretative approach. It was the child of more ordered times.

Pluralism

Dale (1986: 75) defines pluralism as follows:

> Pluralism is a theory of the distribution of influence over decision-making in society. If systems analysis is chiefly concerned with how particular policies are made, modified and implemented, pluralism is concerned rather to know which groups contribute to the decisions, and with why those policies and not others are made. Where one focuses essentially on the nature of the distribution of power within the wider society, the other is interested in the nature of the political *process*.

Pluralists argue that the predominant characteristic of western society has been that a large number of non-overlapping groups have access to and wield political power. It is not the monopoly of a single group or class. Hence there are a number of points or interactions at which political decisions can be made: central and local government, trade unions, business groups, consumers, politicians and many others. Pluralism sees the distribution of power as the predominant characteristic of society (and, by implication, a value in itself and a justification of western societies). Critics of the theory point out that groups can only compete over matters already on this political agenda.

The power actually to create that agenda lies in the hands of a very small number of groups. Again, not unlike systems theory although to a lesser extent, the considerable concentration of political power seen in Britain in the 1980s makes pluralism less useful as an analytical tool with which to explain that very process and its origins – and likely destination.

Marxism

I have already warned that there is virtually no agreement about what constitutes a Marxist approach to education policy making, and Dale reinforces that caveat. The essentials seem clear, however. First, capitalist societies are unavoidably divided into classes on the basis of economic exploitation – that is, the desire of those who own the resources to retain control over them. Second, the role of the state is to maintain economic and political stability. Third, any institutionalized opposition is rendered harmless, partly by being confined to parliamentary institutions and also through the atomization of society into individuals, so that collective attempts to change the distribution of control over resources are impossible or ineffective.

This boils down to four propositions, which clearly have considerable potential value in trying to understand education policy making and control:

1 Inequality in a capitalist society is *structural*, not accidental.
2 The state is not neutral; in general, it will act to support the capitalist economy.
3 The economy sets limits to what can be done in society.
4 Therefore, some problems are beyond the reach of education to solve, and education policy will always be constrained both economically and politically.

Neo-liberalism

We have characterized this position several times already, also describing it as neo-conservatism, or the new right. Liberalism is used here in the classical sense of nineteenth-century *laissez-faire*.

Neo-liberalism builds its critique of the welfare state on two pillars of belief: that the market is more effective than planning; and that individual freedom has been reduced as a result of the action of state institutions. In a pure form, such a philosophy would force the state into the most minimal of roles, as advocated, for example, by Nozick (1975). But the new right in Britain and other countries has taken a pragmatic stance and has set conditions to the market through state controls, so as to achieve other political ends besides the strictly libertarian. That is, the right may engage in social engineering as freely as the left, and thus the neo-liberal does not have to abdicate all power over society. The market itself can be controlled and manipulated and used as a tool for social change. 'Through adjustments in the costs and benefits of any behaviour, individuals can be persuaded to decide to do what is in the "national interest"' (Dale, 1986: 79). Controls over teachers' salaries, the curriculum, and the size and balance of higher education are examples of such regulation of the market.

As we have seen, many of the apparent contradictions in the actions of the new right governments of the 1980s and early 1990s – the use of both free-market forces *and* central controls simultaneously – can be explained by this view of neo-liberalism, and also as a reflection of the power struggle between purists of market theory and centralizers (that is, pluralism *within* the Conservative Party). Neo-liberalism, as a theoretical framework, offers explanations, but they are descriptive rather than analytical: they reveal why those who think in this way act as they do, but little more. Since it is as much an active political and economic philosophy as a theoretical position, this is not surprising.

GENERAL REFLECTIONS AND OTHER EXPLANATIONS

Although these four theoretical frameworks give us various standpoints in thinking about what happened in the educational revolution 1976–92, they do not move us forward. Systems analysis and pluralism are, for the moment, irrelevant; Marxism gives some deep insights but is not fully satisfactory; and neo-liberalism is a description of a prevailing political philosophy which explains neatly why things happened as they did in the 1980s, but not what the social and economic origins or consequences may be. In these closing pages, we shall try to look forward. These speculations are not offered as a contribution to theory or even prophecy, but as ways of focusing the debate which must take place, unless the British remain content to have their children's education controlled in the most drastic and undemocratic manner. As I explained in the Introduction to this part, they derive from reflection upon action, and belong in the western, tolerant and sceptical tradition of historical thought.

Looking back over the story of British education in the twentieth century, it is clear that the predominant control mechanism, besides regulation through public finance, has been public examinations at 16+ and 18+. Until the 1960s and 1970s, these were underpinned by examinations at 11+. The new national assessment arrangements at 7+, 11+, 14+ and 16+ are a drastic reassertion of the general pattern. The purpose was at each stage to admit a reduced percentage of the age-group into the next and more prestigious stage of education. Although everyone might have entered school at age 5, by 18+ only a few remained. The effect was to maintain a mandarin class and to give that class the levers needed to change the quantity and direction of flow of talent.

Before the Second World War, less than 3 per cent of the age-group entered higher education. By 1960, it was 6 per cent; in 1970, it reached 13 per cent, where it stayed until the late 1980s, when decisions were made to expand higher education in the interests of having a more highly skilled workforce. By 1990, it had reached 20 per cent (government projects 28 per cent in 1995 and 32 per cent by 2000). But at the same time, the 'gold standard' of the A level was maintained, and much of the expansion occurred in vocationally oriented courses where entry was allowed with fewer than the minimum two A levels required for a mandatory award or on other criteria. In other words, expansion and elitism were contrived together.

The alternative way to run an education system is not to provide dams and sluices which *stop* people getting to the next stage, but to try to accredit as many as possible by finding and certificating what they know and can do. This is technically represented in the examinations process by emphasizing criterion-referenced testing rather than norm-referencing. In the first, anyone good enough may reach the standard set; in the second, the standard relates to a predetermined proportion of the age-group. The attempts to introduce some element of the first into GCSE have led to accusations of falling standards and to piecemeal government interventions.

Thus the history of post-war education can be seen from one point of view as the gradual erosion of the 'fixed pool of ability' and 'fixed social need for highly trained personnel' schools of social control, and their replacement by those who thought human talent was more considerable and more multifarious than traditional views admitted, backed by those who saw that a modern economy, to be successful, needed to enfranchise a much higher proportion of its people into the educated and vocationally trained echelons. Within this process were carried also the movements to open education more widely to women, those with disabilities and those disadvantaged by class or racial prejudice.

It seems clear that the neo-liberal, new right way of accommodating this tide of widened educational opportunity is by breaking it up into differentiated parts. Whereas the project of the common primary school and the comprehensive secondary school was to give differentiated education according to individual need *within* a common social experience, the neo-liberal project of a market in schooling is based upon differentiated schools and hence a separation of social as well as educational experience. It represents a reassertion of social control through a selective education system, presented as a response to parental choice. What parents actually want most is an excellent school near to their home. What the market offers is choice which is rich or poor according to social or geographical situation and various accidental factors, but where those with money, mobility and knowledge of how to work the system have the greatest opportunities. It can be seen as a massive assertion of self-interest by the middle class, which had felt its grip loosening as comprehensive secondary education proved, contrary to folklore, in so many places very successful.

For the moment, therefore, despite the appalling prospect of a failing economy and social unrest through disenfranchisement of the poor, unemployed and socially disadvantaged, the British do not seem to have been able to break away from their atavistic belief that to be worth anything education must be rationed. The pre-eminence of an elite culture is protected through independent schools, A levels and Oxbridge. The attempt is made to prevent economic failure by providing for National Vocational Qualifications (NVQs) and an expansion of higher education, but within a culturally impoverished context. The preservation of the middle class is assured, together with their power to manipulate the system through grant-maintained schools, assisted places at independent schools, and the powers devolved to schools generally (where the smallness of scale and prescribed responsibilities allow for only the assertion of self-interest by the school). Both the Conservative tradition of 'one nation' and the socialist search for social justice are apparently provided for in the common National Curriculum and assessment arrangements. In reality, the National Curriculum will be hollow unless backed up by differential funding in favour of the disadvantaged (the social priority project), whereas the additional funding has been channelled towards the better-off through, for example, the subsidies given to grant-maintained schools (the differentiation of educational opportunity project).

One conclusion is that the educational reforms of the 1980s and early 1990s are far from being the revolution claimed. The pain and dislocation might be worth it if they were. The new right's underlying agenda, not surprisingly, is the preservation of those parts of the status quo which they value and the taming of disruptive elements in society which may threaten them. In the end, the so-called reforms turn out to be deeply conservative in the dictionary sense, to the point of being reactionary. Control has been gathered at the centre because a national economic and social crisis was perceived, within the context of Britain becoming a subset of Europe. The reform programme was dressed up in the trappings of individual freedom and the Citizen's Charter: but in reality it is a charter for only some citizens.

Why? Why is education used mainly as a form of social control in Britain, rather than as liberation? We have seen that Marxists would expect it to be thus; pluralists would regret it, but point to the great gains none the less achieved and hope for a return to better times; Conservatives would be glad of it.

No doubt thousands more words will be written to try to explain why. One thing is clear to me. The English have never achieved, as a people, a sense of the *democratic intellect* in the way, for example, that the Scots have, or the French. John Knox ordered that there should be a schoolhouse by every kirk. The ability to read the Bible for oneself was a tenet of Calvinism. Protestantism in England remained much nearer to Catholicism and never evinced a democratic spirit. Dissenters of a democratic frame of mind either emigrated or remained in socially impotent groups. And although our political revolution, in the seventeenth century, was earlier in time than those of other European nations, it only led to a consolidation of hierarchies and classes, not their destruction or a sense that they ought to be removed through time. Thus, never having had a real revolution of either spirit or polity, England remained deeply attached to continuity and past symbols, reinforced by a caste system. Efforts to offer education to all as the solvent, though heroic and very successful on the small scale at various times, have always, on the whole, been reined back by a subsequent reaction. For the moment, that programme of providing education as a liberation of spirit and mind and body has been set aside, the more hypocritically because the rhetoric would have us believe that freedom is the purpose.

Another deep reason can also be suggested. There are only two ways of constituting civil society: upon the basis of either person or property. By a civil society based upon person is meant one in which the right to access to whatever is provided collectively is gained solely because the person is a member of that society. The protection of the Greek city state or the medieval village was given equally to all deemed citizens or villagers. The projects to offer equality before the law, or freedom of speech, or the right to vote would be within the same philosophical context. So, pre-eminently, would the National Health Service, the social benefits system, and 'education for all' in the period of the British welfare state. At least in theory, it was only necessary for a person to be a British citizen for that person to be able to claim, and for those providing the service to acknowledge, a right of access. Hence the many attempts to widen opportunity for access and to give disadvantaged persons the means to act on an equal footing or reach an equal starting point with others.

The notion of constituting civil society upon the basis of property takes a wholly different starting point. By 'property' is meant not only physical possessions, but everything an economist might call 'positional goods' – those possessions and attributes that confer advantages (or otherwise) in the market place and social milieu. Among them would be birth, class, race, gender, genetic endowment, inherited wealth and, of course, education. Each of these confers advantage and disadvantage according to the individual within any given social context. Societies constituted upon the basis of property have, of course, been far more common historically: aristocracies, feudal societies and Victorian England, for example, were constituted in this way.

As we have seen, what occurred in the period of building the welfare state, in post-Second World War Britain, was the extension of 'person' into totally new fields such as health, welfare, employment and education.

The neo-liberal project of the 1980s was to transfer the basis of British civil society from person back to property. Everything done by the Conservative governments, not least in education policy, is understandable in this light. It is a gigantic gamble. The advent of the 'knowledge society', in which what people know and can do will be the determinants of economic and social success, actually requires a stronger collective code of behaviour – a higher sense of morality and responsibility for others. And that needs in the first place to be rooted in the individual. Unlicensed individualism would lead to economic breakdown. This truth appears to be dawning upon government, but the 'solution' asserted, of a return to religious morality of a primitive kind, offers no countervailing force to the unbridled individualism of the market place, which is encouraged in all other respects. A sense of the individual's responsibility for others, that we are 'all part of the main', cannot be grafted as an excrescence upon individualism. It must be a deep moral imperative, integral in the development of the individual personality and the social mores. If we are ever to become an open and successful society, at peace with ourselves and effective in a world economy, the liberal agenda for education – the enfranchisement of all into the polity – will have to be revived.

LAST THOUGHTS: YOU AS TEACHER

All this analysis may have either depressed you or stimulated you: or done both at different times for different reasons. I started this book with the processes by which you would get your first job. And I want to end it by saying that, quite simply, the most important controls are in your own hands. It will be the day-to-day relationships that you create with 'your' children that will quicken or deaden them – and you. The curriculum is built as much out of the methods and styles of teaching and learning as from the 'content', thought of as knowledge, understandings and skills directly taught. And that web of ways of working, the respect accorded individuals, the ethos of the classroom, all lie in your hands and within your power to charge with meaning and significance so that the children feel both cared for and stretched, both given respect for what they are becoming and expected to give respect to others for what *they* are becoming. It is the most challenging and also the most joyful of tasks to be a teacher. The joy and the challenge

173

need to be given first to the children: then they will grow also in you.

Central government policies for education since 1979: landmarks

The nature and origins of the ideas of the new right

Conflicts within the new conservatism:

- 'old conservatives' emphasized efficiency, accountability, the removal of power from socialist LEAs and would accept centralization for these purposes;
- 'new radicals' emphasized the market, freedom of choice, an end to producer domination and a minimum of central control over the curriculum

Position of the DES:

- critical OECD Report (1975);
- falling school rolls;
- need for retrenchment;
- concern over curriculum, etc.;
- more power required at centre

Theoretical perspectives:

- systems theory
- pluralism
- Marxism
- neo-liberalism

Salient characteristics of education in Britain:

- predominance of academic élitism and 'fixed pool of ability' ideas, yet partial success for widening educational opportunity leads to conflict between ideas for a common experience of school (comprehensive education) and separate development;
- new right emphasizes differentiation between schools rather than within schools – problems this raises if National Curriculum is to be seen as a common entitlement, and for social cohesion in a pluralist society

Speculations on possible reasons for education being used in Britain more to control than to liberate

Differing conceptions of the basis of civil society: the reversion from 'person' to 'property' in the 1980s

A message to you as a teacher

Bibliography

ACAS (Advisory, Conciliation and Arbitration Service) (1986) *Teachers' Dispute ACAS Independent Panel: Report of the Appraisal Training Working Group.* Mimeo, ACAS.

ACSET (Advisory Committee on the Supply and Education of Teachers) (1984) *The In-Service Education, Training and Professional Development of School Teachers.* London: DES.

Alexander, R. (1984) Innovation and continuity in the initial teacher education curriculum, in R. Alexander, M. Craft and J. Lynch (eds) *Change in Teacher Education: Context and Provision since Robbins.* Eastbourne: Holt, Rinehart & Winston.

Audit Commission (1989) *Losing an Empire and Finding a Role: The LEA of the Future.* Occasional Paper no. 10. London: HMSO.

Baron, G. and Howell, D. A. (1974) *The Government and Management of Schools.* London: Athlone Press.

Beloe Report (1960) *Secondary School Examinations Other Than GCE.* London: HMSO.

Board of Education (1941) *Education after the War.* ('Strictly Confidential'. The Board of Education planning paper.)

Brooksbank, K., Revell, J., Ackstine, E. and Bailey, K. (1982) *County and Voluntary Schools* (6th edition). London: Councils and Education Press (Longman).

Brown, T. and Morrison, K. (eds) (1990) *The Curriculum Handbook.* London: Longman.

Browne, J. D. (1979) *Teachers of Teachers: A History of the Association of Teachers in Colleges and Departments of Education.* London: Hodder & Stoughton.

Burgess, T. (ed.) (1986) *Education for Capability*. London: NFER-Nelson.

Campbell, R. J. and Neill, S. St J. (1990) *Thirteen Hundred and Thirty Days: Final Report of a Pilot Study of Teacher Time in Key Stage 1 Commissioned by AMMA*. Education Department, University of Warwick. Coventry: University of Warwick.

Campbell, R. J. and Neill, S. St J. (1991a) *The Workloads of Secondary School Teachers: Final Report to AMMA*. Education Department, University of Warwick. Coventry: University of Warwick.

Campbell, R. J. and Neill, S. St J. (1991b) Submission to the National Commission on Education, December 1991. Education Department, University of Warwick. Coventry: University of Warwick.

Campbell, R. J., Little, V. and Tomlinson, J. R. G. (1987) Public education policy: the case explored, *Journal of Education Policy* (special issue) **2**(4).

Campbell, R. J., Evans, L., Neill, S. St J. and Packwood, A. (1991) *Workloads, Achievement and Stress: Two Follow-up Studies of Teacher Time in Key Stage 1*. Education Department, University of Warwick. Coventry: University of Warwick.

Caston, G. (1971) The Schools Council in context, *Journal of Curriculum Studies* **3**(1), 50–64.

CATE (Council for the Accreditation of Teacher Education) (1985) *Criteria for the Accreditation of Courses of Initial Teacher Training*. London: CATE.

Chilver Reports (1988, 1989, 1990 and 1991) *First, Second, Third and Fourth Reports of the Interim Advisory Body on School Teachers' Pay and Conditions*. London: HMSO.

Chitty, C. (1992) *The Education System Transformed*. Manchester: Baseline Books.

Cooke, G. and Gosden, P. (1986) *Education Committees*. London: Longman.

Crowther Report (1959) *15 to 18: Report of the Central Advisory Council*. London: HMSO.

Dale, R. (1986) Perspectives in policy making, in the third-level course, *Module I: Introducing Education Policy: Principles and Perspectives*. Milton Keynes: The Open University.

DES (Department of Education and Science) (1972a) *Teacher Education and Training* (The James Report). London: HMSO.

DES (1972b) *Education: A Framework for Expansion*. White Paper. Cmnd 5174. London: HMSO.

DES (1975) *A Language for Life* (The Bullock Report). London: HMSO.

DES (1977a) *A New Partnership for Our Schools* (The Taylor Report on governing bodies). London: HMSO.

DES (1977b) *Education in Schools: A Consultative Document.* Green Paper. Cmnd 6869. London: HMSO.

DES (1977c) *Curriculum 11-16.* London: HMSO.

DES (1978a) *Primary Education in England: A Survey by HMI.* London: HMSO.

DES (1978b) *The Composition of Governing Bodies.* White Paper. Cmnd 7430. London: HMSO.

DES (1979a) *Aspects of Secondary Education in England: A Survey by HMI.* London: HMSO.

DES (1979b) *Local Authority Arrangements for the School Curriculum.* London: HMSO.

DES (1979c) *Curriculum 11-16.* London: HMSO.

DES (1980a) *A Framework for the School Curriculum.* London: DES.

DES (1980b) *A View of the Curriculum: HMI Matters for Discussion II.* London: HMSO.

DES (1981) *The School Curriculum.* London: DES.

DES (1982) *The New Teacher in School.* London: HMSO.

DES (1983a) *Curriculum 11-16: Towards a Statement of Entitlement.* London: HMSO.

DES (1983b) *Teaching Quality.* White Paper. Cmnd 8836. London: HMSO.

DES (1983c) Circular no. 8/83: The school curriculum. London: DES.

DES (1984a) Circular no. 3/84: Initial teacher training: approval of courses. 13 April.

DES (1984b) *Parental Influence at School: A New Framework for School Government in England and Wales.* Cmnd 9242. London: HMSO.

DES (1984c) Press notice no. 85/84: More influence for parents at school. 23 May.

DES (1985a) Press notice no. 70/85: Better schools.

DES (1985b) Press notice no. 74/85: Secretary of State's statement to the House of Commons, 26 March.

DES (1985c) *Quality in Schools: Evaluation and Appraisal.* London: HMSO.

DES (1985d) *The Curriculum from 5 to 16.* Curriculum Matters 2: An HMI Series. London: HMSO.

DES (1985e) *Better Schools.* White Paper. Cmnd 9469. London: HMSO.

DES (1986a) *Better Schools Evaluation and Appraisal Conference, 1985, Proceedings.* London: HMSO.

DES (1986b) Circular no. 6/86: Local Education Authority Training Grants Scheme: financial year 1987-88. August.

DES (1987a) *School Teachers' Pay and Conditions Document 1987*. London: HMSO.

DES (1987b) *The National Curriculum 5–16: A Consultation Document*. London: DES.

DES (1987c) Press release no. 11/87: Kenneth Baker looks at future of education system. 9 January.

DES (1987d) Press notice no. 22/87: Kenneth Baker calls for curriculum for pupils of all abilities. 23 January.

DES (1987e) Press notice no. 115/87: Legislation next Parliament for a National Curriculum: two new working groups announced in Maths and Science. 7 April.

DES (1988a) *School Governors: A New Role*. London: HMSO.

DES (1988b) *The New Teacher in School*. London: HMSO.

DES (1988c) Circular no. 5/88. Local authority training grants.

DES (1989a) *School Teacher Appraisal: A National Framework*. Report of the national steering group on the school teacher appraisal pilot study. London: HMSO.

DES (1989b) *Developments in the Appraisal of Teachers: A Report by HM Inspectorate*. London: HMSO.

DES (1989c) Circular no. 24/89: Initial teacher training: approval of courses. 10 November.

DES (1989d) *Report by HMI on the Implementation of LEATGS: Report on First Year of the Scheme, 1987–88*. London: HMSO.

DES (1989e) Circular no. 5/89: The Education Reform Act 1988: the school curriculum and assessment. 22 February.

DES (1989f) Circular no. 20/89: Local authority training grants.

DES (1990) Administrative memorandum no. 1/90: The treatment and assessment of probationary teachers. 20 April.

DES (1991a) Circular no. 10/91: School teachers' pay and conditions of employment. 26 June.

DES (1991b) Circular no. 12/91: School teacher appraisal. 24 July.

DES (1991c) Letter from R. D. Horne: School teacher probation. 17 September.

DES (1991d) *School Teachers' Pay and Conditions Document 1991*. London: HMSO.

DES (1991e) *School Teachers' Pay and Conditions of Employment*. London: HMSO.

DES (1992a) Press notice no. 96/92: Clarke announces major changes for new teachers. 4 March.

DES (1992b) *A Report by HMI: The Induction and Probation of New Teachers, 1988–91*. London: DES.

DES (1992c) *Curriculum Organisation and Classroom Practice in Primary Schools: A Discussion Paper* (The Alexander, Rose and Woodhead Report). London: DES.

DES (1992d) *School Teachers' Pay and Conditions Document 1992.* London: HMSO.

DES (1992e) *School Teachers' Review Body: First Report 1992.* Cm 1806.

DFE (Department for Education) (1992a) *Choice and Diversity: A New Framework for Schools.* White Paper. Cm 2021. London: HMSO.

DFE (1992b) Administrative memorandum 2/92: Induction of newly qualified teachers. 11 August. London: DFE.

DFE (1992c) Circular no. 9/92: Initial teacher training (secondary phase). 25 June.

DoE (Department of the Environment) (1972) *The New Local Authorities: Management and Structure* (The Marshall and Bains Reports). London: HMSO.

Evans, A. and Tomlinson, J. (eds) (1989) *Teacher Appraisal: A Nationwide Approach.* London: Jessica Kingsley.

Fiske, D. (1975) *Education – The Cuckoo in the Local Government Nest.* Lady Simon of Wythenshawe Memorial Lecture. Manchester: Manchester Education Committee.

Furlong, V.J., Hirst, P.H., Pocklington, K. and Miles, S. (1988) *Initial Teacher Training and the Role of the School.* Milton Keynes: Open University Press.

Glickman, B.D. and Dale, H.C. (1990) *A Scrutiny of Education Support Grants and the LEA Training Grants Scheme.*

Goodyear, R. (1992) *The In-Service Curriculum for Teachers: A Review of Policy, Control and Balance.* Policy Analysis Unit, Education Department, University of Warwick. Coventry: University of Warwick.

GTC (General Teaching Council) (1992a) *The Induction of Newly Appointed Teachers – Recommendations for Good Practice.* London: GTC.

GTC (1992b) *Proposals for a Statutory General Teaching Council for England and Wales.* London: GTC.

Hadow Report (1926) *The Education of the Adolescent.* Report of the Consultative Committee to the Board of Education. London: HMSO.

Hadow Report (1931) *The Primary School.* Report of the Consultative Committee to the Board of Education. London: HMSO.

Hadow Report (1933) *Infant and Nursery Schools.* Report of the Consultative Committee to the Board of Education. London: HMSO.

Harland, J. (1984) The new INSET: a transformation scene, *Journal of Education Policy* 2(3).

Haviland, J. (ed.) (1988) *Take Care Mr Baker!* London: Fourth Estate.

Heller, H. with Edwards, P. (1992) *Policy and Power in Education: The Rise and Fall of the LEA*. London: Routledge.

HMSO (Her Majesty's Stationery Office) (1969) Royal Commission on Local Government in England 1966–69 (The Redcliffe-Maud Report). Vol II, *Memorandum of Dissent by Mr D. Senior*. Cmnd 4040–1. London: HMSO.

ILEA (Inner London Education Authority) (1976) *The William Tyndale Junior and Infants Schools*. Report of the Public Inquiry by Mr Robin Auld QC into the teaching, management and organization of the William Tyndale Junior and Infants Schools, Islington, London N1 (The Auld Report). London: ILEA.

Jones, A. (1989) The real aims of TVE, *Education* **173**(15), 14 April.

Joseph, Sir Keith (1976) *Stranded on the Middle Ground*. London: Centre for Policy Studies.

Kavanagh, D. and Seldon, A. (eds) (1989) *The Thatcher Effect: A Decade of Change*. Oxford: Clarendon Press.

Knight, C. (1990) *The Making of Tory Education Policy in Post-war Britain 1950–86*. London: Falmer Press.

Lawton, D. (1980) *The Politics of the School Curriculum*. London: Routledge & Kegan Paul.

Lawton, D. and Chitty, C. (1988) *The National Curriculum*. Bedford Way Papers 33. London: Institute of Education, University of London.

Maclure, J.S. (1968) *Educational Documents, England and Wales, 1816–1968* (2nd edition). London: Chapman & Hall.

McNair Report (1944) *The Supply, Recruitment and Training of Teachers and Youth Leaders*. London: HMSO.

McNay, I. and Ozga, J. (eds) (1985) *Policy-Making in Education: The Breakdown of Consensus*. Oxford: Pergamon Press/Open University Press.

Merson, M. (1989) Exploring the reform of in-service: TRIST in three authorities, *Oxford Review of Education* **15**(1).

Merson, M. (1992) The four ages of TVEI: a review of policy, *British Journal of Education and Work* **5**(2).

Moore, R. and Ozga, J. (eds) (1991) *Curriculum Policy*. Oxford: Pergamon Press/Open University Press.

Morrell, D.H. (1963) The freedom of the teacher in relation to research and development work in the area of the curriculum and examinations (Address to NFER, 24 October 1962), *Educational Research* **5**(2).

NAHT (National Association of Headteachers) (1991) *Guide to School Management*. Harlow: Longman.

Nisbet, J. (1973) The Schools Council, United Kingdom, in

CERI, *Case Studies of Educational Innovation.* Vol. I: *At the Central Level.* Paris: OECD.

Nozick, R. (1975) *Anarchy, State and Utopia.* Oxford: Blackwell.

Open University (1986a) *Module 1, Course E333: Introducing Education Policy: Principles and Perspectives.* Milton Keynes: Open University Press.

Open University (1986b) *Module 2, Course E333: The Policy-Makers: Local and Central Government.* Milton Keynes: Open University Press.

Plaskow, M. (ed.) (1985) *Life and Death of the Schools Council.* London: Falmer Press.

Schools Council (1981) *The Practical Curriculum.* Schools Council Working Paper 70. London: Methuen Educational.

Select Committee on Education and Science (1970) *Session 1969-70.* Vols I-V: *Teacher Training.* London: HMSO.

SEO (Society of Education Officers) (1973) *The Education Officer and the Structure of the Education Service in Local Government.* London: SEO.

Smith, W. F. Lester (1942) *To Whom Do Schools Belong?* Oxford: Blackwell.

Sofer, A. (1992) Week by week, *Education* **180**(6), 103, 7 August.

Spens Report (1938) *Secondary Education with Special Reference to Grammar Schools and Technical High Schools.* Report of the Consultative Committee to the Board of Education. London: HMSO.

SSEC (Secondary Schools Examination Council) (1941) *Curriculum and Examinations in Secondary Schools.* London: HMSO.

Statutory Instrument (1991) No. 1511: The education (school teacher appraisal) regulations.

Stenhouse, L. (1983) *Authority, Education and Emancipation.* London: Heinemann.

Tomlinson, J. (1981) *The Schools Council: A Chairman's Salute and Envoi.* London: Schools Council.

Tomlinson, J. (1982) *The Profession of Education Officer: Past Pluperfect, Present Tense, Future Conditional.* Sheffield Papers in Education Management no. 25, Sheffield City Polytechnic.

Tomlinson, J. (1986a) *Crossing the Bridge: Addresses to North of England Conferences 1978 and 1986.* Sheffield Papers in Education Management no. 54, Sheffield City Polytechnic.

Tomlinson, J. (1986b) Public education, public good, *Oxford Review of Education* **12**(3).

Vaizey, J. (1963) *The Control of Education*. London: Faber & Faber.

Wilson, M. (1985) *Epoch in English Education: Administrator's Challenge*. Sheffield Papers in Education Management no. 39 (2nd edition). Sheffield: Sheffield City Polytechnic.

Wrigley, J. (1970) The Schools Council, in J. Butcher and H.B. Pont (eds), *Educational Research in Britain*. Vol. 2. London: University of London Press.

NAME INDEX

Arnold, Matthew 63
Auld, Robin 122

Bains, M. A. 156
Baker, Kenneth 85, 155
Baron, G. 121
Beveridge, Sir William 164-5
Browne, J. D. 6
Bullock, Lord 74
Burgess, T. 70, 76
Burnham, Lord 5, 20

Callaghan, James xi, 73, 75, 77,
    110, 121, 158
Campbell, Jim 59, 60, 153
Carlisle, Mark 77
Caston, G. 73
Chilver, Lord 50, 60, 103
Clarke, Kenneth 102, 155
Cooke, G. V. 151, 153
Crosland, Anthony xi
Crowther, Sir Geoffrey 72

Dale, Roger 165-8
Day, Sir Graham 60

Easton, David 165
Eccles, Sir David xi, 72
Evans, A. 101-2

Fiske, Dudley 150
Furlong, V. J. 12, 16

Glideswell, Lord Justice 133
Goodyear, R. 114-15
Gosden, P. 151, 153

Harland, Janet 115
Harman, Grant 165
Haviland, J. 87-8
Hayek, Friedrich von 156, 160
Howell, D. A. 121

Name Index

James, Lord 8
Joseph, Sir Keith 82, 85, 99, 102, 129, 163-4

Kavanagh, D. 161
Knight, Christopher 164
Knox, John 171
Kogan, Maurice 165

Lambert, John 45
Lawton, D. 88
Lockwood, Sir John 72

MacGregor, John 102
Maclure, Stuart 87
McNair, Sir Arnold 6
Major, John 15
Merson, Martin 82, 114
Montaigne, Michel Eyquem de 144
More, Thomas 144
Morrell, Derek 73

Neill, Sean 59, 60
Newsom, John x
Nisbet, J. 72-3
Nozick, R. 168

Parris, Matthew 85
Patten, John 85
Pile, Sir William 151

Plaskow, M. 7
Prentice, Reg 151

Redcliffe-Maud, Lord 150, 156
Robbins, Lord x

Schön, Donald 107
Seldon, A. 161
Senior, Derek 149-50, 156
Short, Edward 8
Simon, Lady 150
Smith, Lester 123
Sofer, Anne 155
Spens, Will 70
Stenhouse, Laurence 5

Taylor, Tom 78, 121
Thatcher, Margaret 3, 8, 15, 77, 85, 109, 158, 161, 162
Tomlinson, J. 73, 101-2, 146-7

Vaizey, John ix, x, xi, 143-4

Weaver, Sir Toby 21
Whitehead, A. N. 68
Williams, Shirley 110, 112, 124
Wilson, Martin 146
Wrigley, J. 73
Wykeham, William 120

Young, David (Lord) 81

SUBJECT INDEX

Advisory Committee on the
Supply and Education of
Teachers (ACSET) 13, 14, 17,
112–13, 118
Advisory Committee on the
Supply and Training of
Teachers (1972) 11
Advisory, Conciliation and
Arbitration Service
(ACAS) 101
appraisal of teachers 95–106, 117,
162
  Education (School Teacher
  Appraisal) Regulations
  1991 35, 44
  National Steering Group
  Report 102–3, 106
  pilot study 96, 101, 106
  report of six teacher
  organizations 104
apprenticeship-style teacher
training 17, 20
area training organizations
(ATOs) 8, 10, 19
assessment arrangements
(National Curriculum) 90

assisted places, at independent
schools .170
Association of County Councils
(ACC) 127, 150–1
Association of Education
Committees (AEC) 150–1,
156
Association of Municipal
Authorities (AMA) 150–1
attainment targets 90
Audit Commission 127, 148,
156–7
Auld Report 122, 139

Bains Report (1971) 156
Better Schools, White Paper (1985)
74, 82–4, 93, 97, 100, 106,
113–14, 118, 125, 127–30,
139
Black Paper (1969) xi, 78
block grant, to local
government 108, 152, 156
British and Foreign Schools
Society 120

Bryce Commission and Report
(1895) 4, 5, 19, 154
Bullock Report (1975) 74
Burnham Committee, Reports
of 7, 19, 49, 60, 150

Calvinism 171
Catholicism 171
Central Advisory Comittee for the
Certification of Teachers
(1928) 6
Chief Education Officer
(CEO) 105, 137, 150-1, 155
Children Act 1989 157
Chilver Reports (1988-91) 50, 56,
103
Choice and Diversity, White Paper
(1992) 147, 154
Citizen's Charter 171
city technology college (CTC) 95,
132, 162
civil society, notions of 172-3,
174
Cockerton judgment 66
community and school 129, 149
Composition of Governing Bodies,
The, White Paper (1978) 139
comprehensive secondary
education 71, 122, 170
Conservative Party manifesto,
1987 86
core subjects 90
'corporatism', in local
government 149, 150
Council for National Academic
Awards (CNAA) 9, 10, 11
Council for the Accreditation of
Teacher Education
(CATE) 14, 15, 17, 18, 19
Crowther Report (1959) 72, 78

cultural diversity 89, 123
curriculum 11-16 (1977-83) 75,
78, 83, 88
curriculum 5-16 (1985) 83-4, 88,
93
Curriculum Organisation and
Practice in Primary Schools
(Report, 1992) 38
Curriculum Study Group (1962) x,
72-3, 78

democratic intellect, the 171
Department for Education
(DFE) 18
see also entries under DFE
Department of Education and
Science (DES) 31, 34, 49, 74,
96, 115, 163-4
OECD Report on 163
see also entries under DES
Department of Employment 81-2,
111
Department of the Environment
148
DES Administrative Memorandum
1/83 34
DES Administrative Memorandum
1/90 32, 35
DES Circular 14/77 77, 79
DES Circular 6/81 127
DES Circular 8/83 83, 93, 127
DES Circular 3/84 14, 19
DES Circular 6/86 118
DES Circular 5/88 115-16, 118
DES Circular 5/89 89-90, 93
DES Circular 18/89 34
DES Circular 20/89 116, 118
DES Circular 24/89 17, 19, 34
DES Circular 10/91 56
DES Circular 12/91 103, 105, 106

DES-LEA-school partnership 77, 83, 148, 151, 155, 164
DFE Administrative Memorandum 2/92 44, 46-8
DFE Circular 9/92 17-19
Dissenters 171

Education: A Framework for Expansion, White Paper (1972) xi, 9, 109-11, 118
Education (Further and Higher Education) Act 1992 156
Education (Grants and Awards) Act 1984 113-14, 118
Education (No. 2) Act 1986 100, 106, 118, 125, 129-34, 139
Education (Schools) Act 1992 139-40, 154, 156
Education Acts
  1870 120
  1902 66, 78, 154
  1944 6, 70-1, 77, 89, 120, 132, 139
  1980 125, 139
  1981 92-3
Education Bill 1978 124-5, 139
Education Committee (statutory requirement) 153, 156
'education for capability' 67, 70, 75-6, 78, 81
Education in Schools, Green Paper (1977) 74, 77, 78, 80, 110, 118
Education Reform Act 1988 25, 26, 85, 88, **89**, 90, 93, 131, 139, 152
Education (School Teacher Appraisal) Regulations 1991 35, 44
Education Support Grants (ESG) 100, 114, 153, 156

Elementary Code (1904) 64, 78
employment protection legislation 34
ethos (of school) 134, 173
exclusions from school 138

Fisher Act, 1918 4
'fixed pool of ability' 169, 174
foundation subjects 90
Framework for the School Curriculum, A (1980) 80-1, 93

'Geddes Axe' 4
General Certificate of Secondary Education (GCSE) 39, 92, 143, 169
General Teaching Council (GTC) 19, 20, 21, 36, 45, 46
  see also Teaching Council
governing body, school 31, 49, 57, 90, 92, **119-39**
  annual report to parents 139
Grants for Educational Support and Training (GEST) 44, 114-16, 118
Great Debate (1976-77) 118
Greater London Council 152
Green Paper (1977), Education in Schools 74, 77, 78, 80, 110, 118

Hadow Reports (1926, 1931, 1933) 4, 67-70, 76, 78

Handbook of Suggestions for the Consideration of Teachers and Others Concerned in the Work of Public Elementary Schools (1905) 65, 78

Her Majesty's Inspectorate (HMI) 18, 26, 27, 29, 30, 36, 38, 39, 40, 41, 42, 43, 44, 63, 72, 81, 83, 97, 107, 118

homosexuality, and the curriculum 136

House of Commons Select Committee for Education, Science and the Arts (ESAC) 21

induction of teachers 43–6

industrial tribunals 34

Inner London Education Authority (ILEA) 122, 132, 152, 156

INSET 107–18
  see also professional development of teachers

Interim Advisory Committee on Teachers' Pay (1987–91) 50, 60, 103

James Committee (1971) Report (1972) 4, 8, 9, 19, 108–9, 118

'knowledge society', the 173

Local Authority Arrangements for the School Curriculum (1979) 77–8

local education authorities (LEAs) 26, 27, 31, 33, 34, 35, 37, 44, 57, 66, 72–3, 74, 85, 86, 90, 92–3, 96, 98–9, 107, 110, 112–13, 115, 120–39 *passim*, 144–5, 146–57 *passim*

Local Education Authority Training Grants Scheme (LEATGS) 114–15, 118

local government 148–57 *passim*, 161
  finance 152–3

Local Government Act 1972 150

Local Government Commission (1968) 149

local management of schools (LMS) 134, 138, 140, 156, 162

McNair Committee and Report (1944) 4, 6, 7, 8, 18, 19, 108

managers, school 123, 139
  see also governing body

Manpower Services Commission 81–2, 111, 118

'market' approach to schools 127, 153, 155–6, 160–1, 168

Marxism and education policy 165, 167, 168, 174

Ministry of Education 71, 72

National Advisory Council for the Training and Supply of Teachers (1944) 7, 19

National Council for Vocational Qualifications (NCVQ) 17, 170

National Curriculum, the 20, 26, 33, 38, 44, 62–3, 74, 82, **85**, 90, 92–3, 105, 127, 135–6, 159, 162, 171, 174

National Curriculum 5-16: A Consultation Document (1987) 86, 93
National Curriculum Council (NCC) 38, 91-3
National Employers' Organization for School Teachers (NEO) 57
National Society, the 120
National Union of Teachers (NUT) 124
neo-liberalism, and education policy 165, 167-8, 174
'new magistracies' 131
'New Right' Conservatism 148, 160-2, 164, 170-1, 173
 see also neo-liberalism
newly qualified teachers 46-8
Newsom Report x

OECD Report on DES (1975) 163, 174
Office for Standards in Education (OFSTED) 118

Parental Influence at School: A New Framework for School Government in England and Wales (1984) 125-7, 129, 139
parenthood 89
parents 119, 121, 123, 125, 128
 complaints and appeals by 137, 162
partnership, *see* DES–LEA–school partnership
PGCE (Postgraduate Certificate in Education) 9, 12, 15
Plowden Report x
pluralism, and education policy 165, 166-7, 168, 174

political balance in school curriculum 136
politicization of education 121
Post-war Reconstruction (1944 White Paper) 4
Practical Curriculum, The (1981) 81, 93
Primary Education: Suggestions for the Consideration of Teachers and Others Concerned with the Work of Primary Schools 66
Primary Education in England (1978) 74, 78
probationer teachers 32, 33, 37, 39, 40, 41, 42, 43
professional development of teachers (INSET) 95, 99, 107-18, 162
programmes of study 90
Protestantism 171
public examinations 16+, 18+ 169

qualified teacher status 13

rate-capping 156
Remuneration of Teachers Act 1965 60
Revised Code (1863) 63, 78, 94
Robbins Report x, xi
Ruskin Speech, James Callaghan's, 1976 xi, 63, 73-5, 78, 110, 118, 121, 158

school boards (1870-1902) 120

School Curriculum, The
(1981) 81, 93
school day, length of 136
school development plan 117
School Examinations and
Assessment Council
(SEAC) 93
School Teachers' Pay and
Conditions Act 1991 56, 137,
139
School Teachers' Review Body
(STRB) (1992) 56, 60
schools
controlled 49, 95, 131
county 49, 95, 131
grant-maintained 139, 153, 162,
170
special agreement 49, 95
voluntary-aided 49, 95, 132-3
Schools Council x, xi, 72-3, 78,
81, 93
Schools Funding Agency 153-5,
162
Scottish Education Department
46
Scottish General Teaching
Council 46
'secondary education for all', aim
to provide 107
*Secondary Education in England,
Aspects of* (1979) 74, 78
Secondary Schools, Regulations for
(1904) 66-7, 78
'secret garden', the 72
secular curriculum 135
sex education 136
social control 171
Society of Education Officers 86,
151
Spens Report (1938) 70, 78
systems theory, and education
policy 165, 168, 174

Task Group on Assessment and
Testing (TGAT) 93
Taylor Committee and Report 78,
121-6, 139
Teacher Training Letter 7/84 19
teachers' associations and trade
unions 96, 104, 148
teachers' duties (1987-) 51-5
*Teachers' Pay and Conditions
Document*
1987 50, 60
1992 56, 60
Teachers' Pay and Conditions of
Service Act 1987 49, 50, 60,
148
Teaching Council for England and
Wales 11
see also General Teaching
Council
Teaching Quality (1983 White
Paper) 13, 14, 19, 97, 106,
111-13, 118
Technical and Vocational
Education Initiative
(TVEI) 81-2, 93, 111, 114,
118
TVEI-related in-service training
(TRIST) 114, 118
Tyndale Junior School ('Tyndale
Affair') 122, 139

View of the Curriculum, A
(1980) 81, 93

Weaver Report (1970) 21
welfare state, the 165, 167, 172
White Paper (1944), *Post-war
Reconstruction* 4

White Paper (1972), *Education: A Framework for Expansion* xi, 9, 109-11, 118

White Paper (1978), *The Composition of Governing Bodies* 139

White Paper (1983), *Teaching Quality* 13, 14, 19, 97, 106, 111-13, 118

White Paper (1985), *Better Schools* 74, 82-4, 93, 97, 100, 106, 113-14, 118, 125, 127-30, 139

White Paper (1992), *Choice and Diversity* 147, 154

Winchester School 120